APPALACHIAN
REVIEW

**VOL. 51, NOS. 1 & 2
WINTER & SPRING 2023**

**50 YEARS OF
TRADITION. DIVERSITY. CHANGE.**

EDITOR
Jason Kyle Howard

BOOK REVIEWS EDITOR
Emily Masters

STUDENT ASSISTANTS	MANUSCRIPT READERS
Lie Ford	Katherine Scott Crawford
Soul Nwaokoro	Patti Frye Meredith
Ian Williamson	

ADVISORY BOARD

Richard Hague	Lee Smith
Marc Harshman	Lyrae Van Clief-Stefanon
Maurice Manning	Neela Vaswani
Karen Salyer McElmurray	Crystal Wilkinson

ESTABLISHED IN 1973
www.appalachianreview.net

©2023 by Berea College. Vol. 51, Nos. 1 & 2, Winter & Spring 2023. All rights reserved. No part of this publication may be reproduced without the prior permission of *Appalachian Review*. Periodicals postage paid at Berea, Kentucky, and at additional mailing offices. ISSN# 2692-9244 (Print); ISSN# 2692-9287 (Digital).

The short stories in this publication are works of fiction. Names, characters, places, and incidents are either the products of the authors' imaginations or are used fictitiously. Any resemblance to actual events, locales, or persons, living or dead, is entirely coincidental. The views expressed in the creative nonfiction herein are solely those of the authors.

Electronic submissions only at www.appalachianreview.net. Distributed through a partnership between the University of North Carolina Press and Duke University Press. Basic subscription price: $32/year for individuals, $62/year for institutions. For subscription requests and inquiries, visit the magazine's website, email subscriptions@dukeupress.edu, or call 888-651-0122 (toll-free in the US and Canada) or 919-688-5134.

CONTENTS

EDITOR'S NOTE .... *Jason Kyle Howard*   6

SPECIAL FEATURE
CREATIVE NONFICTION: FAMILY MATTERS
Ann Pancake
   Yellow Jackets 9
Jarred Johnson
   A Shipment to Rabbit Run 45
Sarah Ladd
   Checking Out 86
Nancy Luana Wilkes
   Wildwood Drive 117

FICTION
Jeff Wallace
   Relief, Relief 21

POETRY
Terry L. Kennedy
   Transformation, or the Idea of It 18
   Yesterday, the Rain 19
   One Kind of Remembering 20
Emry Trantham
   Why We Went to Sliding Rock in April 41
   Every Time 42
   Appalachian Inheritance 43

Dorothy Neagle
- *Black Bird Red* 66
- *Arson* 67
- *Ode to the Cocklebur* 69

Faiz Ahmad
- *Reborn* 81
- *Sunset Photographers* 82
- *The Old Telephone Pole* 83
- *After Spinoza* 84

Josh Nicolaisen
- *My Bluebird* 94

Burnside Soleil
- *Shelby* 95
- *Jeremy* 97

Jeff Tigchelaar
- *Whitman Spent a Summer Wrestling Trees* 113

Ashley Danielle Ry
- *I Think They Call This* Hero Worship 115
- *Consider All Possible Etymologies of* Charm *in* Southern Charm 116

Sara Jeanine Smith
- *My Mother's Madame Alexander Doll* 129

Cecilia Durbin
- *Bernadette* 131

Alison Terjek
- *Coping, Outside the Lines* 136
- *Celebration of Lights* 137

INTERVIEW

Jason Kyle Howard
- *Patricia L. Hudson* 70

CRAFT ESSAY
Richard Hague
    The Jar & The Beetle (& The Rhinoceros)............................ 99

BOOK REVIEWS
Alison Turner
    In the Hands of the River by Lucien Darjeun
    Meadows.. 132

CONTRIBUTORS 139

COVER PHOTOGRAPH
Winter Coats. Cotton Candy Sky. by Carey Neal Gough

EDITOR'S NOTE

JASON KYLE HOWARD

In the early 1970s, Appalachian poet Albert Stewart had a mission. He saw a gap: Appalachian literature was thriving, but Appalachian writers needed a place to showcase their work. The past few years had seen departments and centers devoted to various identities—including Black, women, Latino and Appalachian— spring up on college and university campuses across the country. Against this backdrop, Stewart founded *Appalachian Heritage* in 1973.

This year the magazine, now called *Appalachian Review*, is celebrating that legacy: fifty years of remarkable writing, of promoting emerging voices, of complexifying the identities of Appalachia and its people. We've come a long way since our founding. Over the years, the magazine has published the winner of and finalists for the Pulitzer Prize, finalists for the National Book Award, as well as winners of the T. S. Eliot Award, the E. B. White Award and an O. Henry Prize. Some of our contributors are—or have become—well known and established voices, while others are emerging writers, some of whom are being published for the first time in our pages. We take pride in all of them, and in the contribution they are making to literature from and about this region.

This double issue features work from a group of remarkable writers, including a special creative nonfiction section about family from acclaimed novelist Ann Pancake and emerging writers Jarred Johnson, Sarah Ladd and Nancy Luana Wilkes. Jeff Wallace offers complex characterization and startling description in his short story "Relief, Relief." Noted poets including Terry L. Kennedy, Emry Trantham, Faiz Ahmad, Alison Terjek and others contribute poems of undeniable depth and power. Richard Hague, a longtime contributor to the magazine, offers a craft essay that explores new ways and methods of "paying attention." In our conversation, debut novelist Patricia L. Hudson talks about her approach to historical fiction and how she crafted the character of Rebecca Boone, whose story has been largely subsumed by the fame of her husband Daniel.

As we mark our golden anniversary, I'd like to reaffirm our commitment to Appalachia and its writers. We seek to present the region in all its complexities. We want to lift up and celebrate stories and voices from marginalized communities.

We aim to represent an Appalachia defined not just by place but also by spirit, including urban, diasporic and comparative literature.

This issue is a toast to our first fifty years—to the work of all our contributors, to the vision and commitment of our previous editors. Here's to them. Here's to you, as always, for reading. And here's to fifty more years. ■

YELLOW JACKETS

ANN PANCAKE

Seems you were born closer to an edge than the rest of us were. Seems you knew it too.

Seems maybe that was why, the bitter night you were born, you fought so hard against coming out. We roller-coasted fifteen miles of mountain road to the Richmond hospital at 3 a.m., and there you balked. "Turned funny," the doctor said after all the wrenching and twisting, your birth the hardest of our mother's six. "He was turned funny," our mother'd say later, one of her twenty explanations for your "problems."

When you were a baby, I was eight years old and already caring for kids. When I changed your clothes, your diaper, I'd stop and rub the little knot in your lower belly. I'd press on it. You'd just gaze back. A hernia, what you got for fighting being born. You came home already hurt that way.

■ ■ ■

By the time you were six, I'd seen you almost get killed at least twice. That of course didn't count the ones I wasn't there to see, but I was there for this:

A snowy Sunday afternoon, you about five years old, me twelve. The six of us doubled up on our sleds, a little one riding on a big one's back: you on Sam, Jimmy on Catherine, and Laura on me bringing up the rear—our sleds tied in a train to the pickup's back bumper. I remember quivering with excitement, I can feel the stretch of my mouth in its terrified grin, and our father guns the truck.

Then we're crashing through the pasture, exhaust in our faces, spewed snow in our teeth, Laura's arms choking my ribs, me gripping the sled crossbar for life. We are slamming grass hummocks, lifting, sailing, crashing back to the ground, the ecstatic reckless, the glorious out-of-control. Through slitted eyes, I see the fenceline coming, the scrub trees snow-hunched along it, I feel our father turn the wheel.

You flip off Sam and into the air.

I watch Catherine and Jimmy's sled carve over your head. We're screaming at our father, STOOOPPP!!!, but already my sled's on you, I see you under me, your hat lost, my runners skidding your blond skull, my stomach passing over your body, then you're gone ....

Our father finally brakes. We're springing off our sleds and sprinting to you, are you crushed, did we murder you?—but you are already staggering to your feet. You shake off your arms, you look down at yourself, and you are saying, not yelling, saying, so it's more to yourself than to us, and I hear the surprise in your voice: "I'm okay. I'm okay."

■ ■ ■

The place we grew up was forty acres of ways to kill a kid. The South Branch River. Mill Creek. Abandoned outbuildings. Route 50. The woods. The train. The trestle.

My rescue nightmares started when I was a teen. Often, you, Jimmy, and Laura were in a bathtub together, laughing and playing, unaware that you're all bleeding to death because your legs have been chopped off at your thighs. In an even more common one, we're at the mouth of the creek behind our house, a hundred yards downstream of the trestle, and for a second, I glance away, and you or Jimmy slip in. I look back to see you turning over and over under water, your limbs rigid, a plastic doll. I crash into the creek and before I get to you, I wake up.

Strangely, in my trestle dreams, only I am in danger. A railroad trestle spanned Mill Creek a hundred yards from our house, tall as a church counting the steeple. The ties about eight inches apart, wide enough to terrify a kid with a view of the shallow creek below; close enough together that you couldn't fall through. But the trestle had no railings, no sides. You could sure fall off. Still, the trestle was a vital shortcut, not using it to cross the creek meant long steep detours elsewhere. So we used the trestle anyway to get where we needed to go.

In my trestle nightmares, the gaps between ties are so wide I have to jump between them. Most often, I get to the middle and find the whole rest of the bridge has dropped off, but I'm moving too fast to stop my fall.

■ ■ ■

This happened a couple years after the sled incident, but I didn't know about it until Catherine confessed to me twenty years later. Catherine, ten, coerced you, seven, into a secret adventure involving a rope and a nearly vertical mountainside above the pasture. She told you to wait at the bottom, then climbed that hill face herself, and I can feel it, I climbed there often. The hemlocks and dogwood angling out, the limestone juts, Catherine would be relying on hands as much as feet. When she got pretty high, she threw down one end of the rope and told you tie it around yourself.

"I actually pulled him almost to the top before it happened," she said. The knots you'd made around yourself gave. "I was scared to death, but all I could see was this orange jacket rolling over and over, bouncing off rocks and trees and logs. I was sure he was dead." She shakes her head. "I have no idea why he never told on me."

Another time, you weren't yet two. I heard you wailing from a bedroom where you were supposed to be taking a nap. I found you on your knees in this old basinette, a hand-me-down my parents got who knows where, your head stuck in a hole in the netting. I rushed to you. Grabbed the netting and wiggled you free, your hot scalp under my hand, perspiration-damp, and the tears and the snot. I realize now you weren't in real danger of strangling, but I sure didn't realize that then.

■ ■ ■

You're nineteen for this one. It happened, like they say wrecks do, just a quarter mile from home. You blacked out in the back seat of a drunk friend's car, the friend passing a semi on a Route 50 curve. The force of the guard rail slamming the door snapped your thigh before you were catapulted out, one finger nearly ripped off somewhere in that flight. Sometimes I imagine it like my eyes were implanted in the ceiling, watching you in murky slow motion: your leg buckled in metal, your snapped femur piercing your jeans, you sailing from there into the dark. But somehow your head stayed safe, your spine; just the broken leg and that finger, and even the finger rescued by a strip of skin. The next day, one of your drug buddies showed up at the house with your ballcap in his hands. He'd fetched it out of the hillside honeysuckle where you'd landed.

After the wreck come the decades of all the edges we're not there to see. The ones we are forced to imagine, to dread, to await, to hear about from others, to be lied about by you, to piece together, to guess. One's breath held always, the arrest, the dealer or buyer vandalizing or robbing the house, the fatal car accident, the overdose. For thirty years I've anticipated the phone call telling me you finally crossed the edge.

■ ■ ■

You told me this story yourself, one of those biannual conversations we've had during our adult lives. Your son Lucas was four at the time, so you must have been thirty-five. You and Lucas had been heading out of the woods through the hollow behind the house where you squatted. Early evening late October, day chilling down. You just happened to catch sight of some kind of insects mobbing the bottom of Lucas's jeans, and when you kneeled to swat them off, you realized they were yellow jackets, sleep-walking, sluggish from the cool, but somehow still able to swarm. Then you saw them coating your own calves too, and you panicked, you swept up Lucas and sprinted to the house, scraping off bees as you ran.

As you told me this, you pulled Lucas closer on your lap. "But neither of us got stung."

■ ■ ■

This edge is from Lucas's perspective, him about three. I'm behind our parents' house pushing him in circles on a Barbie Big Wheel our mother found at a yard sale. You're thirty yards away "fixing" the roof of the detached garage, which is exactly what you were doing when I was here three months earlier. The garage stands at the back of the yard, its roof even with the elevated railroad embankment about ten feet from it. I'm bent over Lucas, my hands on top of his on the handlebars, running in dizzying laps, Lucas cackling with glee—when we hear the sightseeing train.

The tourist train that runs daily in fall for the leaf colors. The chug-roar of the locomotive slowly gathering speed after braking at the crossing over Route 50. Now we can see it passing over the trestle at about the speed of a person at a trot, and my mother is calling, "Look, Lucas, look! Wave, Lucas, wave!"

But Lucas has slammed down his feet to stop the Big Wheel. His eyes are fixed on the garage.

"Wave, Lucas, wave!"

Lucas scrambles off the Big Wheel so fast it tips over. "Da! Da!" he yells. He runs a few paces towards the garage, pointing at you. "Da! Da!"

Now Lucas is racing full-tilt towards you, his finger pointing and I chase after him, trying to understand his distress. Then he halts, his arms outstretched: "Da! Da!" I drop on my knees, loop my arm around his shoulders, and down here, I suddenly see what Lucas does.

From his vantage, the garage roof is flush with the railroad tracks—the actual gap between the building and the bank invisible—so that you on the roof are kneeling directly in the locomotive's path. For Lucas, the train accelerates, you ignore it, the engine bears down, it's within a couple body lengths of smashing your back, I grasp all this in an instant and pull Lucas to me, "It's okay. It's okay," right as the train passes directly behind you, jolting everything back into proper perspective.

Lucas heaves under me. He does not cry. In the noise of the train and the nail gun, you never heard him. The cars hurtle behind you, tourist faces gawking. You pretend they aren't there.

■ ■ ■

By the time you're forty, your front teeth have softened and browned. By forty-five, your teeth are gone. Your thryoid is obliterated by thirty-eight, your esophagus eroded from "having nothing to do but lie down after I ate" in jail. Your hands haven't stopped shaking since 1991, and fist-sized knots mushroom behind your knees. Some months you're swollen big. Other months you're filed down flat.

Your friends, your acquaintances, your customers, your dealers, die. Guns, exposure, blacked-out drives, corroded livers, suicide, murder. Overdoses. Overdoses. Overdoses. Overdoses. The brief oblique obituaries. The rumor rumbles that fill those in.

At forty-two, while accompanying your son and all your nieces and nephews into a rinky-dink amusement park, you collapse in the parking lot. Laura gets you to an ER. They rescue you from organ failure.

At forty-three, you go into organ failure again. Again the hospital saves you.

A few weeks before you turn forty-five, the Sunday after Thanksgiving 2015, you start to die in Laura's old bed in the upstairs of our childhood home. I see the ruined mattress later, smeared and soaked with blood and shit, but at the time, only my mother and Lucas are there. My mother does not call an ambulance because you "might get mad," until Lucas, fourteen, forces her to. That time you're in intensive care for ten days.

That particular night of edge, I was 3000 miles west. I won't learn what happened for three more days. But the night it did happen, I woke up stark, and this dream had no pictures, just a naked voice in my head: "There's been a death."

But there wasn't.

■ ■ ■

The time I saw you come closest, I remember what you were wearing. Sears Toughskin burgundy jeans. Tennis shoes. No shirt. You were five or six, so I must have been twelve or thirteen. Our father—we always needed money—was trying to sell a piece of property on the other side of the creek. He and the attorney who was interested walked across the trestle to take a look, and some of us kids followed.

I can smell now the railroad tie creosote, an odor viscous and almost tart. I smell the summer creek below us, comforting to me, algae and rock, minnow and mud. The trestle ties are spaced so that if you are a bigger kid, you can hit a rhythm and cross them two at a time. If you are little, short-legged, like you were that summer, you have to take them at a stutter, one by one. Either way, the only way anyone can make it is by close control of where you look—and by not thinking too much. That muggy boring summer afternoon, we tail our father and the lawyer over, look at the land, turn around, and cross back.

I'm almost to the end of the trestle when I glance over my shoulder. Why I turn, I do not know, because you aren't making a sound.

You're alone in the middle of the trestle. Your knees high-kicking, your elbows wings, your silent mouth bawled open. I understand instantly: a yellow jacket nest. You pitch towards one unrailed edge, reel back, careen to the other side—catch yourself there. Your wrists flail, your legs jig, your naked belly, your small self against the long curve of track behind you, the rocky thread of creek a million feet below. And me—I'm paralyzed. I can't run to you without using my eyes to place my feet—but I can't take my eyes away from you about to fall.

You are my little brother. I cannot reach you. Once again, you hold the edge. ■

TRANSFORMATION, OR THE IDEA OF IT

It matters: the difference between noticing
a muskrat, its barely-visible wake, versus
the quick-ripple of the water snake on the otherwise
flat surface of the river's horizon.
In other words, it could not be ignored,
the difference, nor could its implications:
I was frightened as should be expected.
Without fear, what is love? Without
love, for that matter, what do we
notice? The smallest things, those we live on
inside of, are always, without fail,
awaiting re-discovery. They are like
small children lost in a game of hide-n-seek;
which is to say, with the desire to be found
and, therefore, not hiding at all, not really.
A way to practice loss, you called it.
Then, I agreed. But now, I see differently,
see transformation—or the idea of it: how an exercise
becomes habit, becomes, eventually, such
an integral part of something larger, it ceases
to be itself; the way memory, over time, becomes
more real than the experience recollected: that day
on the river, I wish you hadn't looked at me the way
you did: like someone saying,
This is going to hurt. It's too late to avoid it.

TERRY L. KENNEDY

YESTERDAY, THE RAIN

Yesterday, the rain was quick upon me;
too sudden, too unexpected, to prepare for.
Only the tin of the roof singing—
      less thrum, more heartbeat;
      a hummingbird—
in alarm. It seemed a soundscape
of your leaving: what's not there
more important than what is.
I turned my face to the sky, imagined
a time when the worst has yet to happen:
you are sleeping; I press my ear
to your chest—how steady your heartbeat, how strong.

TERRY L. KENNEDY

ONE KIND OF REMEMBERING

Winter would bring the quiet
of freshly-fallen snow—and what I'd discover,
unexpectedly, in the startling grasp
of a long-dead rose: how there's more
than one kind of remembering. Meanwhile,
summer, meaning the sparrows were,
naturally, singing at cross-purposes; or
at least not in a manner suggesting
call-and-response, much less so, harmony:
a lot of noise; and every bird, to the smallest,
straining to out-do the other—
filling the air with hot-static, then,
something unrecognizable; unrecognizable but
undeniably on the horizon.

TERRY L. KENNEDY

RELIEF, RELIEF

JEFF WALLACE

She'd heated the ham in the fellowship hall that morning. It had been that blue time of the morning, and the swamp in front of the church was still chirping with frogs. She had let herself into the side door of the church—it was a vinyl-sided building built like a barn, all white except for its stark black roof and black faux shutters. It was still cool and a slight fog raised off the swamp. The hog farm across the highway hadn't started to stink yet.

Now folks were walking into the communion hall and grabbing what they wanted from the tables. Sue had a Styrofoam plate of ham, mashed potatoes, green beans boiled and soaked in bacon grease, fried sweet potatoes, and two slices of Heiner's white bread. Her ham was cut to the bone already and folks were moving on to the re-heated Kentucky Fried Chicken.

She sat on an aluminum folding chair and felt old. Well, not old, she reconsidered. Oldish. Well...no. Old. She was old, she decided. She was old and her mother was older, and the rest of her family was dead or had moved and she was old. But the church was still here and she could bake a good ham. And Easter was a time of salvation and renewal.

Sue picked at each piece of the meal, tasting and considering. Her ham was good, she knew that. The sweet potatoes could have been browned a bit more. Maybe a touch more brown sugar. The green beans were cooked to mush, but that was how it should be—the grease carried that.

"Lot of dessert up there," Howard said. He was standing on her left. He wasn't sure when he got there. "I made your sister's dump-cake."

She looked up at him from her chair and wiped her mouth with a paper napkin. The plate of food was perched on her crossed legs. "You know, I never cared for it. It's too sweet. And the coconut." She looked back to her plate and took another fork of the potatoes. They were lumpy and could use more salt. You could taste how she used milk instead of cream. Thelma had done a poor job of it.

"It's still awful sweet, but I cut the coconut." he said. He was holding his plate in one hand and had small red Solo cup and fork in the other. "I never cared for it either."

"How's the chicken?" Sue asked.

"Not half as good as your ham." He grinned at her and shook a cold chicken leg. He was still tall, still had that pencil thin mustache, and his hair was still black. "I snuck a bit during the sermon."

That color can't be real, Sue thought. She softened then, thinking of her own yellow hair and how many boxes of dye she had gone through to get the color she was born with.

He'd lost some hair, too, in the fifty years since high school: his widow's peak was deeper than ever. He'd gained some weight, too (hadn't we all, she thought); he moved a bit slower than he did when she had been a cheerleader for the basketball team he played on. She remembered that he had even played sometimes.

"Be careful that the preacher don't see you sneaking off. You're a deacon," she said and laughed.

Coach Whitley had been so tough on the basketball team. Running them up and down the hill outside the school every afternoon before practice. Whitley had coached her son, Travis, for a season. Then Travis had died. Her boy.

The thought had pulled into her mind. You'd think those vacuum-spaces of memory and grief would be easier as years passed. Nearly forty years now. But they came so unexpectedly and they came with so much force that they always sucked the air out of her lungs. No, squeezed it out of you.

Whitley had been old back when her son had played, she thought. Your age now, she thought. Old and dead. The fork in her hand trembled and she stabbed at another bite of the mushy green beans. His age, his death, her boy's death, was like watching house lights going out one at time. Her own lights would be flipped out not too awful long from now.

"I'll just bring him a slice of pie next time he's at the old folks home," Howard said.

"You gonna feed the preacher a piece of cafeteria pie?"

Howard laughed, and pointed with the chicken leg, "Now, no. I can bake. I bake for all the old ladies in the home. I can make a pie as good as my momma's. Daddy said it was better, but I don't believe it."

It was funny: fifty years later, fifty-three years, really, since high school, and Howard was still mostly Howard. And he was still handsome. Handsome for an old man, anyway.

■ ■ ■

"Cook for your own damn self then," Sue said. "I ain't gonna cook again after cooking for the church. You always *have* liked fried chicken and mashed potatoes. I can't help it if it don't taste good right now."

Leonard's legs were weeping through the bandages she had wrapped his feet with. The seep-stained the chair where he sat.

Leonard looked up at her from his recliner. He was a big man. Heavy and trunk-armed. He still had his head of light hair and his bushy yellow beard was streaked with grey.

He'd been so pretty when she'd met him up north. 1972. He had been smoking Pall Malls and playing pool in Defiance, Ohio. She had been singing then. Her band, The Love Strucks, had done two nights there. It was a good place to play—a lot of family had moved there to work in the factories. Those were good shows. They'd opened for The Amazing Rhythm Aces, three years before they got big. The Love Strucks had almost made it. Almost.

"I can't taste for shit," he said. He closed the legs on his recliner and tried to stand up. His weeping, split feet held him there. It was obvious it hurt and he tottered. "Bring me my boots," he said.

"Fine," she said. She went and got his steel-toe boots. She would have called them work boots except that he didn't work anymore. "Where are you going anyway? It's Easter Sunday. Nothing is open. And whatever would be open is closed for Covid."

"Bullshit," he said. "I'm going to Portsmouth. The river helps me breathe. I feel like I can't breathe in here and my feet feel like they want to burst."

"You're crazy. If you catch it, it'll kill you. You can breathe just fine if you'd take your medicine. And your feet are swole up because of your sugar. Just stay, Lenny. The river is thirty minutes away. You can barely stand. Take your medicine, eat some chicken and stay home."

He lumbered towards the door. He had to navigate through the kitchen, into the utility room, and then outside down the steps. She was not going to help.

"I'll eat dinner on the way," he said.

She sat down at the table and ate the dump-cake Howard had scooped for her. Better than her dead sister's recipe, she thought. She could hear Leonard groan and cuss with every step. Part of her hoped he'd fall. Part of her hoped he'd make it to his truck and then just keep driving. That's a good recipe,

> *She could hear Leonard groan and cuss with every step. Part of her hoped he'd fall. Part of her hoped he'd make it to his truck and then just keep driving.*

she thought. A lot less sweet than her sister's. Fresh cherries too. Not the sickly-sweet cherry filling her sister had always bought from the Amish.

Her sister, Teri, had been younger than her, and had been just a kid when The Love Strucks toured. Sue had taken her to as many shows as she could. Sue had even brought her to Defiance for that weekend, the weekend she met Leonard. Sue had been twenty-two. Teri just eighteen.

Yeah, those had been some good days. She remembered Teri getting drunk off Old Milwaukee beer that some old creep had bought her, and how she had thrown up in the bathroom of that bar. What was that bar's name they had been in? After the second night he'd helped them pack up their equipment into their van. He carried the amps like they were nothing. He'd been so strong then. She'd invited him back to the hotel that night and had sent Teri off to the drummer's room for the night. Leonard had been so handsome with his funny northern accent. She thought he'd been like a Viking. Two days later he found them in Toledo and watched for a few days there. Then he just kind of...stuck. Like a roadie. He'd sit in the audience and cheer when she sung. She sent Teri home and Leonard took her spot in the room.

And then Sue was in love.

And then she was pregnant.

And then she'd come home and he'd stuck here, too. She knew he hated it here. But that wasn't her fault and this was her home. So, when she had a baby, she came home. It had been the right thing. For her, at least. And they'd raised Travis the best they could while he'd lived.

She stood and walked to the kitchen sink. She could see him out the window as he walked to his truck. When had she started to hate him? He'd turned so bitter. Cruel. And then he'd gotten sick with the sugar. And you'd think that a person would be grateful for help, but it had only made him worse. Travis had gone. And Lenny had hit her some.

No, she hoped he'd fall. Hoped that he'd drive that car right off the road in Portsmouth and into the river.

She said a quick prayer, asking God to forgive her for that thought. But a part of her still liked to watch him struggle across the gravel drive.

■ ■ ■

Howard always asked her to come out with the rest of the choir, but she always said no. But, for whatever reason, this time when he'd asked during Wednesday night Bible study and choir practice, she had, for some reason, said yes.

Now she was in a bar and grill in Jackson watching folks take turns singing karaoke. She nursed a beer and watched them sing.

Most of the choir hadn't come this week—just her and Howard and Thelma Lou. But she knew the rest of the folks singing. She'd gone to school with some, saw some of them grow up. Patty Stapleton had sung a Shania Twain song. Howard and Doug Adkins (who Howard was still buddies with from high school) had sung together on "Total Eclipse of the Heart." They couldn't hit the high notes but no one cared. The crowd had laughed and cheered as they plowed their way through the song. Thelma Lou, the only other member of the choir, had sung a Willie Nelson song.

"When are you gonna get up there, Sue?" Thelma Lou asked her. She had a halo of salt-and-pepper perm framing her face and bifocals. She was drinking a bright pink wine cooler.

Sue finished her beer and wished for a cigarette. It had been twenty years since she quit (a fiftieth birthday present to herself), but she still felt the pull of it sometimes. At a bar, drinking a beer, listening to folks sing, this was a moment when the pull was strong. "I don't know—I don't mind singing in churches, but I've never sung karaoke before."

"But it ain't like you've never *sung* in a bar," Howard said. "Did you know Sue almost made it big? Right after high school. She was in that band and toured all over the state."

"West Virginia, Indiana and Kentucky, too." Sue wanted another beer. "But who's counting," she laughed.

"Oh yeah, she was gonna be big time. She was great on stage. Like Blondie and Dolly Parton put together."

"What kind of music did you all play?" Thelma Lou asked, leaning forward, adjusting her bifocals. She had graduated six or seven years after Sue and Howard.

Howard answered for her. "Southern Rock. Kinda like the Eagles or Skynyrd. Better, if you ask me."

"Oh my," Thelma Lou said. "Were you ever on the radio?" She sat her empty bottle down on the table.

Sue could feel herself smiling. This was nice. "A few times. We pressed a record and stations would play before we played in their towns. No official fan clubs."

"I still have that record," Howard said. "I don't have a player anymore, but I still have all my old records. I know for a fact that yours is good."

Sue could feel herself blushing. She covered her face with her hands, "Lord, that's embarrassing."

"Now, no. You were really good. It's a good record." There was a pause in the noise of the bar as a singer stopped to a smattering of applause.

"Isn't that something," Thelma Lou said. "I'd never have guessed. You never sing nothing but harmony at church."

Is that so, Sue wondered. Why *didn't* she ever take any of the solos. Her voice was still strong and true. And maybe it was the beer, but she felt Thelma Lou didn't believe her.

"Howard, would you get me another beer?" She started to reach for her purse but he waved her off.

"I tell you what: You go sign up and I'll buy you and Thelma both another drink."

"I don't know," Sue said.

"Jesus turned the water into wine, not milk, Sue," Thelma said. "He wanted *happy* Christians. Just not drunk ones. I'll have one more, but I do have to work tomorrow. High school seniors can sniff out a hungover math teacher."

Still not retired, thought Sue. That was one thing Sue didn't mind about getting older—the freedom over your days that just fell on you when you retired.

Freedom, she thought. That wasn't quite what she felt. She wasn't *not free*, but she wasn't really free either. When was the last time she felt free? The band, of course. Just a few years of real openness, living hand-to-mouth (or voice-to-mouth, really), not quite sure where you were going to sleep. Or with who. And then Leonard. And then Travis. And then all the mess after that. It was like a series of doors and windows that looked out on possibility and inwards to different forms of herself had blown shut in the steady wind of hours, and days. Small decisions that led to big difference and doors slamming soundly shut forever on all the things that could have been. Years and decades of choices that were not, wholly, what she wanted. And the shitter was, she thought, that they'd been the right decisions.

"I'll take a Jack and Coke, Howie," she said. Let's make a bad decision, then.

■ ■ ■

She woke up the next morning with cottonmouth and a headache that seem to start at the bridge of her nose and blossom out from there to cover her entire skull. Even her ears hurt. She hadn't been properly hungover in twenty years and the difference in the memory of that hangover (a Fourth of July party where one of her sister's college-aged sons had brought home a new drinking game that *everybody* had to try), and the feeling of this one were stark. That one had been bad. This one was something else. And her throat hurt. She coughed as she came fully awake, grateful that she had left a glass of water on the coffee table.

She looked around her small living room. A couch, a recliner, a coffee table. A book shelf with just knick-knacks and a picture of Travis at eighth-grade graduation. Goddamn it, she thought. All of it old and worn. She coughed again and took a drink of the water. Her throat definitely hurt. She coughed again and wiped at her nose.

"Lenny, you awake?" she called out. She had her shoes off. "I'm sick."

"Hungover," he called from their bedroom. Well, the bedroom. She'd slept in Travis's old room for the past ten years. "You have fun?" he asked—an accusation. His voice was raspy. He sneezed.

"I did. A lot," she said. Maybe she was still a bit drunk.

She'd started with the one Jack and Coke. Then she'd had a rum and coke. And then, a whiskey sour. That had always been her favorite. She remembered singing. She did the same song as Howard, "Total Eclipse of the Heart," but she'd sung it well enough that people had applauded. And then she'd sung some Patsy Cline. There had been cheers for that. And then she and Howard had sung "Islands in the Stream." His voice had been bad, flat, but it was fun, and she'd clung to his neck in a hug afterwards. And she'd smelled his aftershave on his smooth face and she remembered wondering if he had shaved that evening for her. And then he and Thelma must have brought her home.

"Well, you must've brought something home with you, because I'm sick too," he said.

"Or you brought it in from Portsmouth."

"I'm always by myself, outside, down there. You did this, you bitch." He broke out into a series of coughs, long and rattling, and then moaned.

She walked from the couch, unsteady on her feet. She was still wearing her shoes. They must have dropped her off at the door or just inside it. Maybe she had brought it with her, she thought. Maybe it was from the church. She went to the door of his room.

"I'm allowed to go out. And you need to take care of yourself sometimes," she said. She could smell the sickness on him, and she could smell where he hadn't changed his wrappings on his feet. "Have you eat yet?"

"Not since before you left for Wednesday services. I didn't feel good so I stayed in bed." His big body looked blue in the morning light. The bed sheets and blankets were wadded up around his groin like a loincloth. His body was still impressive: solid as an oak stump, still yet, she thought. But hollow now.

"You were sick yesterday? You knew you were sick and you let me go out?

"I just thought it was my allergies. Just…worse."

"You knew. You son of a bitch. You knew. And you let me go out there."

"We don't know and you're sick too. You brought it to me. I didn't do this. You did. All this. All this is your fault. All of it."

He was staring at her—through her. His beard was flecked with spit. His pale and blue chest had turned pink in his rage. "Every bit of it. From Travis on this has been your fault. And now you're gonna kill me too, just like you did him."

She had always been frightened of Leonard. He was a big man, both inside and out. He could be tender, an endless well of love and care, and it had always felt so good to drink from that well. Not the well of eternal life that the Bible promised, but something close. But there was also the other side of that. The wild anger and violence. Both she and Travis had faced that too much. It was as if her body was being torn in half as she looked at him. She could feel the push and pull of the man, of his love and his anger, the weight of the time blowing open doors closed and the sounds those doors made as they slammed. She felt her own body and face redden with sudden anger, and she was racked by a sudden cough. And then she saw him in the bed, clearly.

The light came through the window in slants. Dust motes spun in the stale air. He was breathing heavy and there was still saliva in the blonde and grey strips of his beard. She could see his teeth. Small, she saw now, clearly, the cloud of closeness and time stripped away. Tiny teeth in a small round mouth. The wild hair of his head and the heaviness of his body, the fear that they brought, were stripped away and she saw him clearly. Just a child in that bed. Raging against his choices. The beard, she saw was ridiculous, almost a glued on thing. His teeth were milk-teeth. A child crying out in the dark. She did not feel pity.

"I didn't kill our boy. I bought him a car. And that was a good thing for a sixteen-year-old boy to have. He died. The truck hit his car and he died. We fought, he got mad, he drove

> *The light came through the window in slants. Dust motes spun in the stale air. He was breathing heavy and there was still saliva in the blonde and grey strips of his beard. She could see his teeth.*

off too fast. And then he died. People just die." The words were heavy as they came out. Heavy and slow and they sunk into the room and into Sue's heart. A weight was not lifted; instead the feeling of a stone weight falling into place.

"No, you killed him. And now you're gonna kill me," he said from the bed. Sue thought he might be crying.

"No, Lenny. I'm not going to kill you. I promise." She walked to him and kissed his forehead, feeling nothing but the heat on her lips from his fever and the coolness that seemed to radiate from her own insides. "You're burning up. Let me get you some water and I'll make some breakfast. Something light. Feed a cold, starve a fever…give a snack to Covid?"

She watched as he changed from that angry child into just a child. He was calm and happy. A toddler. A baby. The rage had all swept away from him. The balled up sheets at his groin were a diaper, not a loincloth.

"You've always been so funny, Susie-Q," he said. An old pet name. She would have shivered from it if she hadn't felt so heavy and hard in her stomach.

"Buttered toast and coffee for both of us. And I'll have somebody run over some tests from the pharmacy. You rest and I'll take care of it."

She made the toast and the coffee, took some Tylenol and then called Howard. He didn't answer so she left him a message.

"Hey, Howard. Lenny and I are both sick. I don't know who caught it first, but it might be Covid. Do you think you could run me out a couple of the tests from the pharmacy? I'd really appreciate it. And you should get tested. So should Thelma Lou." She paused, not sure how to continue. But she remembered how he smelled when they had sung together. She smiled remembering how flat his singing had been. "And thanks for last night. First fun night in twenty years and now I'm gonna die of Covid. So thanks for one last good night, Howie." And then she hung up.

He came out later that evening with four tests and a pot of soup for her and Leonard. He also brought The Love Strucks album.

"I figured since you weren't going to be leaving, you may as well have it to listen to," he said.

"You're sweet, Howard."

■ ■ ■

She felt bad that first day, but she had been able to take care of herself and help Leonard as best she could. The second day, they had gone to the hospital. They had been sent home. Sue with prescription cough syrup and Leonard with antiviral medication.

The three days after that, things were bad.

The second day she ate some, cooked a bit, but she was feverish and coughing hard enough to see stars. She was still able to make food for herself and Leonard. She took the bandages off of his feet and changed them, but poorly. He had gone to his recliner in the little living room and stayed there. The living room, between the kitchen and the bathroom, was a good spot so that he didn't have to walk as far to the bathroom. But the bandages bled onto the foot-rest of his chair.

The third day was worse still. She didn't cook but she was able to get ice water and Tylenol for them both. And Leonard's antivirals. Leonard wasn't raving, but he wasn't always making sense then, either, and he would not take his medicine.

"I just need to breathe," he said. "If I can just get to the river. If I can just get to the water, I can breathe." He'd wrapped his feet on his own in towels, but too loosely. They were old and ratty towels, from when even Travis was still alive. The seams in the towels were ripped and stray strings clung to the thickened blood and blister-water, like seaweed left by the tide.

"You need to take your medicine, Leonard," she said. "If not, I'll need to call the emergency squad to come get you." She hadn't known what time it was when she had got water and had gone to the bathroom.

His eyes hadn't cleared, but he said in a raspy, strangling voice, "If you call the squad, I'll never get out of there alive."

"Okay, Lenny," she had said.

The fourth day she did not leave her bed, but slept and dreamt of Travis. He was so very small in the dream; it was his second birthday—and he had a small trampoline to jump on. He held the bar that attached to it (she had bought it, Leonard had put it together). There were streamers in the corners and cake on the table. Teri was there.

"Watch me, momma! I hop and hop and hop and hop, bunny, bunny, bunny!" His brown hair had been long—they still hadn't given his first haircut.

And then his head had started to weep like the wounds on Leonard's feet. But he didn't notice. He smiled and jumped. And then Leonard had stepped to her. Big, strong, young, Leonard. "This is your fault," Leonard said. His hands were weeping and bleeding and he picked the boy up.

Travis began to scream. And so did she.

■ ■ ■

She woke herself up with her screaming the morning of the fifth day with the sheets in her dead son's room wrapped tightly around her.

One eye was crusted shut, but the one that could open saw that late-morning light was coming through the window blinds. She was hungry, in an irrationally strong way.

"Lenny! You out there?"

She struggled to her feet and teetered through the small room and narrow doorway. She looked into the living room towards where Leonard should be sitting.

The dream had been awful, but the silence of her home was more awful still.

He wasn't there. His cellophane pack of antivirals were next to his recliner. None had been taken since the two she had given him before she had gone into the dark.

"You didn't take your medicine, Lenny," she said. She walked past his empty chair, finding strength now in a surge of anger. "Won't even give yourself medicine. You'd drown in the rain," she said and shuffled to the kitchen.

Beans and cornbread, she thought. That'd be good. She should make that. Sausage and kraut too. She started to pull eggs and milk from the refrigerator before she realized she wasn't thinking straight. I can't cook, she realized. I need water and to sit. And then food. She left the eggs and milk on the counter and tottered back into the living room. She heard the awful silence again and finally her thoughts fell into place. Lenny was missing.

She went back to the kitchen, glanced at the milk and eggs she'd left on the counter and started to put them away. She picked up an egg and the milk jug before realizing again: Lenny was missing. She went from room to room, still holding

She heard the awful silence again and finally her thoughts fell into place. Lenny was missing.

the egg and milk in her hands. Every room was empty. She went back to the kitchen and looked from the window above the sink into the driveway. And there he was, lying in the gravel, his truck door open, and him in front of it.

She went barefoot into the spring sunshine, carrying the milk and the single egg. It had rained during the night and the world smelled wet and ripe. The gravel hurt her feet and she had a memory of running on gravel in bare feet. Teri and her, out to meet their daddy after he came home from the foundry. The iron dust was ground into his skin.

She came to Leonard and stood by him. His feet were still wrapped loosely in the towels. They seemed to be attached by only the crust of the dried weeping. He was breathing, but quick and shallow. His eyes were open but they did not focus on her as she looked down. He held his truck keys in his hand but the interior lights of the truck were off. Battery must be dead, Sue thought. He's been out here all night then, at least.

"You did it this time, Lenny." She thought about trying to move him inside, but his size and her age and health made it impossible. She squeezed the egg gently in her hand, feeling the damp and cool shell in her palm. And, if she were honest, she did not want to move him. "I won't call the squad," she said, and walked back in the house.

She made herself lunch, scrambled eggs, and then went back to bed. She did not dream.

■ ■ ■

She was awakened by a pounding and shouting at the front door. It was dark in the house and there was no way to tell the time. As she moved towards the door, she became awake enough to recognize the voice—it was Howard and he was frantic.

"Sue, are you okay? I called the squad. They're on their way. Answer me, Sue, if you're in there!" She could see the door rattling and the knob twisting as he tried to get in.

"I'm coming," she yelled, surprised at how weak her voice sounded.

She opened the door to Howard in a mask. He was in a suit and tie. It must be Sunday, she realized. Church night. He looked nice. Behind him, laid out neatly on the grass was Leonard. Howard had moved him from the rocks.

"The squad is coming," he said.

"Is that Leonard?"

"I found him laying out in the driveway."

"Is he dead?"

Howard's brow tightened and he glanced at Leonard, then at her and then at the ground. Then, in quiet and even words he said, "I don't know. His breathing is real weak." He was lying to spare her, she realized. The lightning bugs were out and flashing. Tree frogs were screaming at the wood line.

They stood in silence with the dead man just behind them, the porch light casting them both in a thin yellow light. Sue noticed his eyes were closed. She wondered if Howard had done it, but she didn't ask him.

"Do you want to pray?" Howard asked.

"No," Sue said. "No, I don't think I do." She could hear sirens coming. Howard took her hands and began to pray on his own.

■ ■ ■

The hardest part had been calling Leonard's family, what was left of them, in Defiance. Only his sister came down. He hadn't wanted a big ceremony—a closed casket, a simple graveside prayer, and that was it. Everybody had to wear a mask. Most of the church turned out to support her, which was nice, but she didn't need them. Howard did not come. It didn't bother her. Even if they hadn't said it to each other, it would have been awkward and unfair. It was just another thing that marked him as a good man. He knew when to stay away.

There was a time when being widowed at her age would have meant three days of visitors and dozens of family members in her home. But those were long-gone days. When Travis was buried it had been nearly a week. Teri had put most of them in her house. But all that was gone. Shut down, like a crate hammered shut.

After the funeral she went home alone. She spent the days following Leonard's death cleaning. She scrubbed all the hard surfaces in her home. She rented a carpet cleaner and cleaned all the carpets and the furniture. She spent nearly an hour on Leonard's recliner, cleaning where his feet had wept onto it. I'll throw that out soon, she thought. And now there was nothing to do. Nothing to clean, nothing to cook, nothing to *do*. So she sat down.

She sat in her kitchen and looked out the window to where she had left him. The ripped vinyl of her chair poked at her thighs. Her dress was uncomfortable and she pulled off her mask. She'd left him. She could change out of these clothes, she thought, but she didn't want to.

The record Howard had brought by was on the table. She looked at the cover and ran a sharp fingernail along the edge of it. She missed that band. She wondered if she could start a band now. She thought about the days touring and the van and the chaos. She couldn't do *that*, but she could sing cover songs. She could piece something together.

She stared at the cover. There she was. She was so pretty, she thought. Dolly and Blondie all at once, that's what Howard had said. There was a coffee stain on the kick drum. Howard must have done that, she thought. But when? It didn't matter. She knew she shouldn't, but she missed Howard and wanted to call him.

She took the record and went to her stereo. She had to fiddle with the speakers before she got it to play. At first the record was spinning at seventy-eight and her voice came out as high and whiny. But then she set it to the proper speed. Lord, she sounded young. How could that have been me, she wondered. How was that voice ever me? But it was. And she knew it was her, and a part of her leapt at the recognition of herself. So much dust and weight and cobwebs. But there she was. Barefoot in the gravel, singing a song as her daddy came home with the iron in his pores. She hugged her arms to herself and rocked herself back and forth in the sound of her own voice.

When the knock came at her door she had just flipped the record to the B-side. Six more songs out of the past, still true and real. She knew it would be Howard before she got to the door. And sure enough, there he was. He was wearing a light blue T-shirt and jeans. He was holding a brown paper bag in one hand.

"I was gonna call you," she said, lying. But it wasn't much of a lie, she realized; she had wanted to.

"I have the stuff for a whiskey sour if you want a drink."

"I do." The sound of her younger voice came from the living room, singing and crying about young love and young pain, a voice still empty of regret and mourning, a voice still full. ■

WHY WE WENT TO SLIDING ROCK IN APRIL

Because I'd dreamt and dreamt
of water, and parsing no sunken
meaning, took dreams as advice:

swim. Because an empty tourist geotag
is a sacred space, no matter the chill
of its currents.

                Because one summer
our brother jumped from a cliff
into Keowee, and when he bobbed back

up to air, I glimpsed his grin
through my shaking fingers. Because given
the moment back, I'd clutch his hand

with the same fingers, and this time,
I'd jump, too. Because I'm still here,
alive enough

                to dread the cold
at the base of this slick stone,
alive enough to plunge in anyway.

Because when that river water
dazed me, I never even wavered—
I knew that I would swim.

EMRY TRANTHAM

EVERY TIME

How many times while hiking or ambling,
while basking on a log for a moment of breathing
in the speckled light of a forest, how many
times have I startled at the movement
of a creature just beyond the periphery?
The rhododendron, thick and blooming,
blind me to what might also be amidst
the shadowed bramble—gliding deer, searching
squirrel, waiting rabbit—but oh, how I half-
hope each time for a giant mammal of a story.
A lone wolf, a bear cub with mother keeping watch,
or God grant me the glimpse of a panther
the old-timers swear still stalk these hills.
I hold my breath, each time, my eyes
scanning the littered forest floor, searching out
the careless hullabaloo until I catch sight
of it: the scattering leaves, the red belly,
the dark-feathered bird who has once again
fooled me—it's always a goddamned towhee.

EMRY TRANTHAM

APPALACHIAN INHERITANCE

When I ask the woman
who owns the Christmas tree farm
if she's native to these mountains,
she laughs and tells me to listen to her voice.
I'd heard the Northern tinge, but there are only a few
ways to ask where a woman is from.
Florida, it turns out, by way of Chicago,
but she bought this lot in Ashe County in 1986.
Her rebuttal branches out:
You aren't from North Carolina, either, of course.
And it's fair—if her dialect is flat as the western plains,
mine rises only to rolling hills. Still, in my shallow,
slight drawl, I correct her quicker than a herd
of white-tails ruins a crop of young Fraser firs.
I've lived here all my life.
The peaks and valleys of my long-eroded Appalachian
speech would have sung it much sweeter.
With that lilt, she might have heard the hillbillies
who made these mountains home decades before I did:
a woman who ran a library from her living room
in Topton. She loaned books to neighbors
from every congregation in Nantahala.
Her son, who married a young woman from Iotla
after he knocked on her door to sell encyclopedias.
His wife, who tells me still
how her grandmother greeted tears
with a held-out apron: *Cry me a pocketful.*
She might have heard the man
who ran a general store in Valle Crucis
until he sold it to a family called Mast.
Or the husband and wife who tilled

the stony soil of Avery County so long
they grew eight children from it,
the youngest of whom is my grandfather.
I wonder if she might have heard my mother
in 1986—belly swollen, body bundled—
selling Christmas trees beside the road
hours before she heard my first cries:
the wail of new generation calling
these mountains home.

EMRY TRANTHAM

A SHIPMENT TO
RABBIT RUN

JARRED JOHNSON

Until I was ten, my family didn't have a home of our own. My dad built houses, and ours was always the last one he'd finished. We lived there till that house sold, then we moved into the newest one to repeat the process. When a house wasn't ready we stayed in hotels. Our moving boxes remained unpacked, the spaces we lived in bare, clean at all times for the realtor to do a showing.

Heeding mom's pleas for a place of our own and wanting more land and privacy, dad bought a farm at auction in 2004. Our property sat on sixty acres of rolling Appalachian foothills about nine miles north of Somerset in south-central Kentucky. Turning off the one-lane road past a horse pasture and creek bed where cattle cool themselves in summer is my family's driveway: two red brick columns with a plastic sign between them welcoming you to "Rabbit Run Wildlife Management Area."

Like many things in my father's life, Rabbit Run is a time capsule. With a grant he received from the state agricultural department, dad covered our property in Kentucky's native grasses—switchgrass, Big and Little Bluestem, Indiangrass, Prairie Cordgrass—so that looking out my bedroom window on the second story, hardly a neighbor in sight, I saw the same dried reeds and swaying green stems, the briars and thistles that southern Kentucky's earliest inhabitants, the Cherokee and Shawnee peoples, might have seen.

Perched in the open space on the highest hill of the property was our red brick home. Two hundred yards downfield was the enclosure where dad trained beagle hounds to hunt rabbits. A black wooden fence, coated on the inside with chicken wire, trailed the perimeter of the enclosure. Made of thin, galvanized steel arranged in a pattern of hexagonal openings, chicken wire creates a kind of metal mesh through which small animals, namely chickens, or, in my father's case, rabbits, cannot escape.

It was chicken wire that defined my and my father's relationship in the summer of 2017. I had just moved back in with my parents after a year teaching English in Germany. A fellowship program to which I'd applied had denied me. I was restless, lost and unfocused, and I was in love. I had left Dimi, my first boyfriend whom I had been dating six months, in Saarbrücken.

That summer while I sat at home applying to jobs, talking on the phone to Dimi each day, trying to decide what shape my life would take, my dad set off to buy a shipment of chicken wire from a manufacturer in China. He had bought 100 acres across the road from our house, and he wanted a build a second enclosure. He needed seventy rolls of chicken wire for the fence. What he didn't use, he would sell. So he solicited my help.

My father doesn't know how to use a computer. He has no email address. He uses a flip phone he loads monthly with pre-paid minutes from a calling card. He can't open or reply to text messages, and his contact list contains no stored numbers. He writes names and phone numbers in ink on the walls of the mattress store he owns.

Like most Millennials, I was the conduit through which my parents reached the world, the bridge between them and the future, Rabbit Run and everything else.

"Hi there," my first email to Weisy Industries said. I found them one night after comparing companies from a few online searches. They were a wire and cable manufacturer based in Shijiazhuang just south of Beijing in northeast China. "My father is interested in buying a container of black, seventeen-gauge chicken wire. He would like to pick it up in Louisville, Kentucky, USA. Can you help with this?"

By the time I woke, Grace, the alias she used with English-speaking customers, had already replied. "It's quite easy to get the cargo to your plant," she said.

Already the illusion. Nothing separated us. No miles, borders, languages, time zones.

■ ■ ■

I accepted the English-teaching assistantship during my senior year of college in Kentucky. I was placed in Saarbrücken, the capital of Germany's smallest state, a city that butts up against the French border in the west—a path I would walk not far from my apartment had a white painted line on it with the words "Wilkommen" on one side and "Bienvenue" on the other.

Dimi and I matched on Tinder four months after I arrived. He was a second-generation Greek-German in his last year of medical school. Our first date was January 20th. We walked along the Saar River until we grew too cold, then we sat in a café called (in English) "the bakery" with a placeless, metropolitan aesthetic, all earth tones, wood and dark metal. It felt American, and I would return in the coming months to escape when I got homesick.

Later that same day I met up with three Americans to watch Donald Trump's inauguration. My parents had voted for him, though I had mailed my absentee ballot for

Kentucky, stretched sidelong so its full body tapered off thin in the west, a chicken leg, as many call it, was one of the first states filled in red.

Hillary Clinton from the post office near my apartment in Saarbrücken, my first time voting for a Democrat. On election day, I attended a party called "Amerika wählt," *America Votes*. About a hundred of us crowded together in rows of chairs in an open meeting space on the second floor of the modern building that housed the German-American Institute. The election results were projected on a hanging screen behind a short stage. Kentucky, stretched sidelong so its full body tapered off thin in the west, a chicken leg, as many call it, was one of the first states filled in red.

The next morning in the teacher's lounge I would be asked a question for the first time that would come over and over for the rest of my stay in Germany: "What happened?" I would feel, not just as an American, but as a Kentuckian, someone who grew up in a conservative, Christian family in a rural part of middle America, a profound need to find an honest answer.

■ ■ ■

To a small subculture of people who call themselves "beaglers," my dad and our farm are famous. Rabbit Run is one of the most prestigious running grounds for beagles in the country, and my dad is a premier trainer. The enclosure is what makes our farm famous, its density of rabbits.

Each year the United Beagle Gundog Federation hosts its National Runoff at Rabbit Run. It's the Olympics of beagle hunting. People from states as far away as Texas and Maine converge in Somerset to compete on my family's farm. Besides training beagles to hunt rabbits, my dad also judges field trials like this one.

On a field trial weekend I was woken early to the sounds of beagles baying in the thickets outside my window. The dogs went in groups of seven into the fields of our farm, both inside and outside the enclosure. Their bodies poked black, white and brown through the openings in the brush. They disappeared, noses to the ground, tails wagging, in a thicket before emerging seconds later on the other side. Sometimes you caught glimpses of the cottontail rabbit dashing ahead of them. The dogs rarely caught them. The hounds' job was to chase, to move, to clear. The hunter's job was to kill, though a field trial isn't a killing sport; it's about the pursuit.

Dad rode on horseback behind the pack. He carried a small scorecard in his hand. He judged the dogs on how well they stuck to the line of the rabbit. Each time they veered off that line, backtracking, for example, casting out too far, missing a check the rabbit hit or following a ghost line, chasing a scent that never existed, dad marked it. The top four hounds from each heat moved on to the winner's pack to compete for trophies and ribbons.

The legacy of rabbit hunting was passed from man to man in my father's family. A dedication to Martin Johnson, my dad's paternal grandfather, is printed on a wooden sign and nailed to the front gate of the rabbit enclosure. "In loving memory of my grandpa," it reads, my father's words. "Oh how I miss him. Just thinking about him brings a tear to my eye."

I never liked hunting. It felt overstimulating and aggressive. I didn't like the kick of the gun on my shoulder or the loud firing of the shells. I hated the sticktights and burs and ticks that clung to me. The dramatic swings between idleness and high stress irritated and exhausted me.

I empathized with the rabbits. Dad splayed their bodies out on his tailgate. I watched him skin them with a pocketknife and wash their meat clean, so they became all sinew and fiber, red and white and glistening. A deep freeze in my parents' garage held all of dad's wild game in freezer bags labeled by date. At his request, mom pulled them to the countertop to thaw. To me wild game tasted like the farm itself, like the land, all dirt and grass and root.

■ ■ ■

I pulled up the email attachment labeled "Offer Sheet" on my phone one night over dinner. Weisy Industries' teal logo was in the top left corner.

"China sent me the price quote," I told dad.

"What they asking?"

We ate meat and potatoes off Styrofoam plates. He drank water mixed with Gatorade from a reused Sonic cup.

"Sixty-seven per roll. A little over 50,000 all together."

"You got a pen and paper?"

Mom handed him an envelope from the far end of the table.

"If we sell a roll for eighty bucks," he said before trailing off. The plastic window flap on the front of the envelope scratched against the glass tabletop as he crunched the numbers. "We're talking 15,000 dollars profit for everything. Not bad."

He spoke over the evening news, which played in the living room so he could excuse himself when the sports segment came on.

"You can negotiate with them," he said. "Offer sixty. See what they say."

"I'm no good at that."

"I'll be dead and gone one day. You got to learn."

He was shirtless, and his white briefs poked up over the waistline of the khaki cargo shorts he had put on after he showered. His skin was pale, pocked by dark spots, and where muscles once flanked his shoulders and chest, his flesh was now wrinkled, shriveled.

In the bottom right corner of the offer sheet was a closeup photo of three imperfect, black hexagons of chicken wire. The tops and bottoms of each shape were wound together, double-enforced, so that each hexagon shared a border with its neighbors, the lines between them blurred, one shape indiscernible from the next.

"I'll talk to them," I said. "Maybe they'll send us a sample."

■ ■ ■

I went to Germany looking for love. Though I'd been out almost two years in my college town, I'd never been in a relationship. My first dates with men were during a semester in Berlin my sophomore year. Only an ocean outside of home and culture could I explore myself. It's why I returned. To speak a foreign language, to live abroad, to receive a Fulbright English-teaching assistantship, to date a German: it was all an attempt at affluence and worldliness. I wanted to be rich and smart and from nowhere.

I thought I found all that in Dimi. He held some of the dualities I couldn't: equally scientific-minded as creative, balancing knowledge of seemingly every ailment and illness with the time he spent working on illustrations, photography and design. He spoke four languages. Though Dimi and both of his parents were born in Germany, he was often treated like an outsider by white Germans who recognized something foreign in his dark skin and beard, or in the many, clapping syllables of his full name. Perhaps this was what I found most attractive about him. He quipped about German culture, observing its qualities one step outside of it the same way I did growing up gay in Appalachia.

Where I was a hopeless romantic, Dimi stepped apprehensively into our relationship. He didn't want to fall in love with someone who would leave. He couldn't envision a future with a visitor, and he was only beginning to envision a future with a man. When I met him, only his roommate knew he was gay.

Following his pace, our relationship started slowly, but things accelerated at his birthday party in early May. By then, I only had three months left in Germany. A group of ten of his med-school friends and I sat huddled close on the two couches in the living space off his bedroom, some sprawled on the floor. We pulled lukewarm beers from thick plastic cartons where the bottles had been refilled and purchased. Dimi put out a spread of dips and fruit and cheese.

"Das ist Jarred," he told them, and I waved beside him. "Mein Freund," my boyfriend.

It was one of my first times in a fully German social setting. My friends in the city were mostly Americans and other Europeans studying or working abroad. Though I spoke German well, I felt shy and quiet, like a shell of myself compared to my outgoing personality in English. It reminded

Though I spoke German well, I felt shy and quiet, like a shell of myself compared to my outgoing personality in English. It reminded me of being closeted, the way I shut off parts of myself...

me of being closeted, the way I shut off parts of myself at church or in the locker room in high school, anywhere I feared my mannerisms or voice might lead to bullying or homophobia.

I observed his friends as they interacted, finding it difficult to jump in quick conversations among native speakers. It was one of the first times I reckoned with myself as a complete outsider in that place, in that language.

■ ■ ■

My father is a man of rigid routines. Each morning is the same: he wakes before six, showers, eats at Cracker Barrel (turkey sausage, grilled toast, hashbrowns with peppers, onions and tomatoes), then checks his rabbit traps. He roams Somerset looking for its last remnants of wildness, its undeveloped lots, its forested ravines. It's how he stocks the enclosure, how he trains his dogs.

He builds the rabbit traps in the back of his mattress store. They're rectangular boxes made from two-by-fours. An opening at one end contains a breathing hole covered in chicken wire; at the opposite end, a swinging door connects to a metal lever. When pressed by weight, the lever swings the door closed, trapping the rabbit inside.

He sets his traps in fields, thickets, brush piles, off roads. He uses a hunter's eye. No rifle or bullet, but dad can't unlearn what he knows. That a rabbit is an edge species. They thrive where two habitats meet, a field and a forest, food and a place to hide. They move between the two using corridors of cover, brushy fencerows or low-lying grassy strips, the liminal spaces between their two homes. These are the places dad targets. A rabbit must hide, evade.

Cottontails are a solitary species. Unlike hares that burrow in communities in underground tunnels, the cottontail escapes wind and cold in holes alone. It's a borrowed home, often dug by another burrowing animal.

A rabbit has a small home range, between two and six acres, that it rarely if ever leaves. They know this range intimately. It's a survival tactic. They use everything in that space to their advantage: they live off of the land; they hide in it. Like dad, they're creatures of habit. They often follow the same paths.

When dad catches a rabbit, he brings it back to our farm where he lets it loose inside the enclosure. Growing up, he taught me how to unbox them. I stuck my hand in the trap to hold open the door, then dangled the box upside down, letting gravity force the rabbit out. Their bodies were only swaths of airy brown, they moved so fast, hitting the ground, then jolting, running away, their back legs springing them forward into the brush to hide.

Back then it felt fun watching them run. I didn't realize what it meant to separate a rabbit from its home. To lure them, trap them, then plant them down in a place in which they were completely unfamiliar. The beagles were let out of their cages one at a time to hunt. Inside the enclosure, they learned to track the rabbit's scent.

■ ■ ■

The chicken wire sample arrived in a thick manila envelope with bubble wrap coating the inside. When dad got home, he found it on top the kitchen table. He looped his fingers through one open hexagon to pull it out. It was about twenty inches long, folded four times.

I watched him wrangle it in his hands before dinner. He snapped it back and forth rapidly testing its durability, trying to break it. He put the wire under his foot and yanked up on it, trying to pull it apart. He wanted to unravel the hundreds of wound threads, to rupture the structure under his force, rip open a hole. But he couldn't. When he gave up, he lifted his open palms to me to show the white lines surrounded by red where the wire had dug in.

"Good quality," he said. "Let's get a full container."

■ ■ ■

In summer, while the heat pushed people out onto the streets and balconies, seeking shade under the spruce trees that lined the Saar or under table umbrellas with Steine in beer gardens, Dimi's and my relationship blossomed. I taught at school while he finished his thesis. We saw each other most evenings. We swam at the public pool or read next to the Saar or went to Silo, the bar and club named for the smokestack that towered above the underground rooms where DJs spun tracks early into the mornings.

The weekend after the schoolyear ended we booked a bed and breakfast in Bernkastel-Kues along the Mosel river in Germany's wine region. After a wine tasting and dinner, we traversed the hillsides full of grapevines, looking into the valley with the Mosel River and the villages on its banks.

"It looks like the Mediterranean," Dimi said again and again, as though his brain were wrestling the unbelievability of this, bridging the two homes he'd known, Germany, where he'd grown up, and the village in Greece where his family returned each summer to help his grandparents harvest the olives they made into oil.

On the drive home we listened to a playlist of gay music he made: Madonna, Whitney, Britney, even Euro hits I had never heard like La Bouche and Alice Deejay. We sang along as Dimi careened through traffic across lanes on the autobahn. He was a different person than the one I'd first met in January, closeted then and reserved, holding back his feelings out of tenderness and caution.

"Are we just going to break up when I leave?" I asked on the drive.

He thought about his answer. "I don't want to do long distance," he eventually said. "I want someone to hold in my bed at night."

"And what if I moved here? To stay."

In those final weeks together, I started to envision a future with Dimi: our house in a suburb outside Munich, the backyard where we hosted dinner parties. I saw us in art galleries and watching plays, traveling to Greece and Kentucky. When he visited Rabbit Run and met my family, we would sleep together in my childhood bedroom, and through the screen windows we would hear the crickets and katydids and bullfrogs that had lulled me to sleep my whole life.

"I won't let you do that," he said. "If you didn't like it, it would be my fault."

■ ■ ■

I called Grace from the mattress store. Dad and I sat at the folding table he used as a desk. On top of it were phonebooks and calendars, his checkbook, the carbon-copy receipts he wrote out by hand. On the wall behind him, photos of me from high school, University of Kentucky basketball schedules from the last few seasons, a photo of his dad and him as a boy standing over a beagle hound.

Grace talked quickly, tersely, despite a warmness to her voice. Though I had her on speaker, dad often asked what she was saying, unable to make out her Chinese accent.

They would need a deposit, she explained, thirty percent of the total, wired to them to start production. The lead time was twenty days. After we wired the final seventy percent, they would send the shipment. The estimated shipping time from the port of loading at Tianjin to Louisville was forty-five days.

"Do you trust them?" dad asked after I hung up. He was nervous it was a scam.

"I think they're legit. I researched them pretty good."

He nodded. He had to trust everything I said, unable to verify anything for himself, completely helpless in the internet.

The next day I emailed Grace the signed invoice and wired Weisy the deposit from dad's account.

57

■ ■ ■

At the end of the summer of 2017 I accepted a communications job at the German Consulate General in Chicago. Mostly I took the job to stay close to Dimi. While I couldn't yet be physically near him, I could prepare myself for that. I would keep working on my language skills and build up my resume. The Consulate processed hundreds of visa applications each day, and I imagined my own application for a work permit landing on the desk of one of my coworkers in the future.

Dimi and I spoke on the phone during my lunch break most days, those few anxious hours when our time zones and schedules aligned. I felt like I loved him, and it caused me to unravel. We had no future we were working toward, no goal in mind, so every slight disagreement felt like the whole relationship was falling apart.

After some persuasion, he agreed to come visit me in the U.S. He wanted to meet in New York, the place he most wanted to see, but I wanted him to see Kentucky. So I drove home to talk to my parents about it.

I tested the subject first with my mom, who knew Dimi and I were dating. She was taking off her makeup in her bathroom late at night after my dad was in bed. I sat in the armchair beside her.

"I'd like to bring him here," I said.

We looked at each only through the mirror. She circled her eyes with a washcloth and Ponds Cold Cream till two black circles of mascara and eyeliner appeared.

"Talk to your dad about it," she finally said.

He and I were the first to arrive at Texas Roadhouse the Sunday before I headed back to Chicago. We buttered two of the rolls the waiter had left on the table.

"You know my friend Dimi from Germany?" I said.

He nodded.

"Well, he's actually my boyfriend, and I'd like him to see Somerset when he visits."

At the word boyfriend his eyes widened.

"No, JJ," he said, "that's not a good idea."

"I just want him to see what it's like in Kentucky," I tried, "since he's never been to America."

"You can't bring that around here."

We drank our waters then, ate our rolls, held the menus stiff in our hands between us. Eventually mom came in, and we didn't say anything else about it.

That already was here and always had been. *That* had grown up at Rabbit Run. *That* had flushed rabbits from their cover in the switchgrass and pulled minnows from the creek, had stuck *that's* body in the sink hole by the oak tree and plucked blueberries from the bushes *that* planted in the valley.

For the first time since my coming out, I felt a rift growing that day, one that threatened to split more than me from my parents, but me from this place entirely, my home and identity.

■ ■ ■

Roughly 15,000 miles separate the ports at Tianjin, China and Norfolk, Virginia. Traveling at twenty-four knots, an average speed for a massive barge, the trip takes roughly thirty days. First, the ship moves southward in the Pacific Ocean before careening through the Panama Canal and slinking up the U.S. coast.

A direct flight passes between Munich and New York City five days a week. The flight traverses 4,000 miles in roughly nine hours. Moving at 600 miles per hour at 37,000 feet, the plane typically curves northward over England before descending south over Canada's eastern border toward JFK Airport.

Dimi and I checked off the typical tourist attractions in New York—Statue of Liberty, Top of the Rock, Central Park—then one evening his Greek aunt, who lived just north of the city, met us for dinner at garden restaurant just under the Highline in Chelsea where she ordered caviar for the table, my first time trying.

Our final morning in the city, Dimi tinkered in the kitchen making coffee, and I packed my clothes in the living room. The sun was bright off the empty walls of the vacation apartment through the east-facing windows.

I never wanted this job in the first place. It had been forced on me. The sense of obligation I felt to my father was nagging, persistent. I felt guilty: for failing him, for being who I was.

My phone vibrated beside me with a call from a California number I didn't know. I ignored it, but when it came again soon after, I picked up.

"It's Celine," the voice said. I recognized the name. She was the forwarding agent with whom Weisy Industries had connected me. She was a Chinese native living in California, and her job was to get the wire from the port of origin at Tianjin to its final destination in Somerset.

"I haven't received your customs clearance," Celine said. "I need it immediately."

She used terms I didn't know: bond application, BOL, consignee. I put her on speaker to Google ISF, a term she kept repeating: Import Security Filing. It was a document required by Customs and Border Protection to import goods into the U.S.

"We have to file your ISF twenty-four hours before your container arrives," she said. "You're behind. You can be fined 5,000 dollars. Your shipment will be turned away."

My head wrestled the thought: all that work for no wire at all.

"Do you understand me?" Celine kept saying. "Do you understand?"

I never wanted this job in the first place. It had been forced on me. The sense of obligation I felt to my father was nagging, persistent. I felt guilty: for failing him, for being who I was.

My father held a son tight in that place—in Somerset, at Rabbit Run. A son he built. Someone who resembled me. He kept that son there. He wanted to heir that son the legacies he built, calloused, stoic, unyielding. But I was not that son. He was not me.

"Yes," I told Celine. "Yes, I understand."

■ ■ ■

An industrial cargo port resembles a helipad or naval ship, a giant paved landing leaping out into the ocean like an island parking lot. The port of Norfolk has twelve lifting cranes like teal blue, metal towers, fingers grasping at the sky. Shipping containers are stacked together on a cargo ship, often eight containers high. An average ship carries twenty crew members and as many 24,000 containers. The port cranes lift these containers one by one and place them on the tarmac where they wait to be dispatched and loaded onto rail frames to travel to their destinations.

The dark red shipping container in which our chicken wire came was held by customs at the Port of Norfolk to await clearance. In the long journey from Shijiazhuang to Somerset, this was the only moment of rest, when the movement halted, the wire and its momentum static, stuck halfway between its origin and destination, held waiting.

Two days later, after paying a per diem fine of $100, we received our clearance. After traveling by rail from Norfolk to Louisville, the wire arrived at the loading dock at my dad's mattress store latched in its original shipping container on the chassis of a semi-truck. Grace emailed a photo just before it departed.

The 760 wound bundles were stacked in rows six rolls high. Each roll contained 150 feet of wire wound into concentric circles. Stacked on top of each other and held together by plastic wrapping and tape, each roll suggested a kind of potential energy, the certainty that once cut loose from their sleeves, each would expand, explode.

It took my father and one of his employees three hours to unload the full container—so long he was forced to pay a detention fee to the shipping company. He had struggled to envision the reality of it: 760 rolls. Or maybe he just didn't know they weighed 109 pounds each, as stated in the Bill of Lading. By the time the truck was empty, dad and his partner tag-teamed each roll, one on each end, their muscles too wary to bear a roll alone.

The wire, the idea of it, had been born now unto flesh—the texture of it, its weight, made tangible to my dad. Now it was something he understood. This was what it meant to exile me.

In one version of this story, there were four more hands unloading that truck, mine and Dimi's. But we were not there. We were not allowed to be.

■ ■ ■

The last time I saw Dimi was March of 2018. I took two weeks of vacation from the Consulate to visit him in Regensburg in southern Germany where he was finishing the first of three stints of his residency.

He hosted a goodbye party for all the friends he had made in that city. A group of us sat on the wooden benches on both sides of a table in the kitchen of the apartment he shared with two roommates he met online. Sitting in on conversation amongst native speakers, I again felt quiet, shy, unable to interject. And perhaps more than the certainty I was an outsider, I started to know I could not envision a life there. This would always be what I felt. Germany would never feel like home to me, but living there was the only option with him.

That night, after his friends left, I became despondent, quiet.

"What's wrong?" Dimi asked. We lay together in the bed in the room he had subleased. On a nightstand beside us, a giant jade plant with white mold flecking the soil.

"I can't do this, Dimi," I said, and when the words came out, I felt the truth of them in my mouth, our history together, all thirteen months of learning and loving unraveling like a spool of wire.

The hug we shared just before I entered the security line at the Munich Airport was our last.

I parted with a tributary of my life that day, a simulated me who might easily have committed to that relationship, have moved to that country. Some parts of me have still not grieved that loss.

■ ■ ■

It's in a rabbit's nature to circle. Because their home ranges are so small, even when hounded by dogs, when flushed from cover, a rabbit bounds away, outdistancing the beagle, until eventually, after a couple hundred yards, it circles back to the place it began. This is how rabbit hunting works. The hounds bound ahead, starting the chase. The hunter waits back. When the rabbit returns, the hunter shoulders their rifle, aims and fires.

I don't live in Kentucky now, though after stints in Chicago and New York, I have returned to the South, to Wilmington, North Carolina. There is something familiar to this place that I didn't feel in the Midwest or Northeast: the cicadas buzzing electric in the trees at dusk, the circular vowels of Southern voices, the performance of politeness. Though parts of me still long to close the 600 miles between Rabbit Run and where I am, I embrace that I am not the young man trapped there, not the rabbit hunted, haunted by the impositions of my parents' culture and politics and religion.

I am learning the beauty of building an enclosure. I am working on boundaries with my family. We don't follow each other on social media. When we speak to each other, there are rules to how we engage. While we can talk about politics and religion, we can't say things meant to hurt each other. Our goal is to preserve, not damage our relationship.

A boundary can be a form of liberation. In Wilmington, I perform drag as "Coal, the Appalachian Queen." I play in a queer sports league. I recently started dating a new man whom I told my parents about. My mom will visit soon. She said she isn't ready yet to meet him.

Many days I drive by the Port of North Carolina here in Wilmington. Following the roads near the port, this beach town, the swamp, gives way to a different landscape. Everything is paved near the port. The roads are wider. The longleaf pines and cypress that cover the city disappear, as does the sandy soil. Every path is lined by chain-link fences and barbed wire. A port is a liminal space, a transition zone part way between an origin and a destination. Everything converges there to wait. That's the stage of life I'm in.

    I don't know what happened to all the chicken wire my father sold. Some is in a landfill somewhere, I am sure, or decaying under the remnants of a burn pile where grass now grows. Some of it was never used and sits wound up in the bundle in which it was purchased. Much of it lines the perimeters of enclosures, fences, rusting perhaps, doing the job for which it was purchased, even made: holding things in, keeping things out. ■

BLACK BIRD RED

Raven is out in the cherry tree, swallowing busily, disturbing branches, clinging to that which glows, red at the throat. Later, he will come inside, while the sun places a fierce bid for heat in the dying hour, and make a pie crust to cradle the berries and crumble like earth. I'll sit at the kitchen table chewing my red lips over comic books, pretending not to be changed by the transformation. Black wings. Tree climber. Tears beading at corners when the coarse hair of his moustache kisses my mouth goodbye, squinting at the light through leaves, rubbing salt from my eyes. Now that he is gone, I don't know what I will do with my knowledge of the sun. Flour. Butter. Drops of ice water. Turn the oven on.

DOROTHY NEAGLE

ARSON

Tires up to his elbows, the old man
rode his tractor all the way to the
end of our road, turned right off
728 and rolled past the empty
field that used to hold tobacco
with its long leaves green and
broadly wrinkled. He wound along
the pond, sinking into itself, mud
covering all the snapping turtles,
and up the hill with its blind curve,
past the cattle penned on red dirt,
by the stand of trees that marked
the beginning of our property where,
if the wind was down, you could hear
tires on gravel from a mile back
standing outside our house. Some
minutes after he completed this
uninvited visit to impress upon
our mother the wisdom of needing
a man to live—to do right by her
children, to understand what can and
can't be owned under God, and by
whom, and having been refused—
he made the journey in reverse, passing
out of sight into the meadow ringed
with trees where deer and wild
turkeys lingered, and which was
set about, at that time, with great
round bales of hay turning silver
beneath the sun, at which point he
took his cigarette between two fingers

and sent it flying into one. As fire is
silent before it becomes uncontained
I was thankful to find it still smoking,
easy enough to put out, though
we could not shake the trespass of
that old man scorned and
the things of ours he tried to burn.

DOROTHY NEAGLE

ODE TO THE COCKLEBUR

Prickly-fruited poison in the sunflower tribe
invasive of *the daisy family* coating the dogs'
fur, caught on sweaters, knotted in my hair
only denim and canvas impervious

to your lack of care which vessel carries you
into the future. Ever the cuffed ankle, tender
envelope between ribbed sock and opening of shoe
are subject to the closeness of you. I have

picked you from bodies, finger-brushed the crumbling
petals of your shed housings, shook them from damp
unraveled clothes and given up on soft, on delicate—

all woolen things. Still you cling to me, though I was never
enough to hold you. You don't know when the traveler
has gone, only that another will come by to carry you on.

DOROTHY NEAGLE

AN *APPALACHIAN REVIEW* CONVERSATION

PATRICIA L. HUDSON

When she was writing *Traces*, her debut historical novel about Rebecca Boone, Patricia L. Hudson had a goal: to bridge the distance between present and past. "My goal...was to make readers feel immersed in these women's thoughts and feelings, so that you felt as if you were moving through their eighteenth-century world right alongside them," she explains.

Reading the novel, it quickly becomes clear that Hudson more than succeeded. With great skill, she manages to balance deep character interiority with compelling action that propels the narrative forward—quite the feat for a first-time novelist.

Hudson had long wanted to write a novel about Boone. A longtime journalist whose work has graced the pages of magazines including *Southern Living* and *Country Living*, her writing often centered on history: preservation, historic sites and approaching the past with complexity. All the while, her thoughts often turned to Boone, whose story has been largely subsumed by legends surrounding her outsize husband Daniel.

In compelling, lyrical prose, Hudson restores agency to Boone, writing her life with an historian's eye for narrative and detail, and a novelist's instinct for characterization and interiority. She recently spoke with *Appalachian Review* editor Jason Kyle Howard about how she approached *Traces*, the erasure of women in historical narratives and how she dealt with the Boones' role in colonialism and Manifest Destiny.

■ ■ ■

JASON KYLE HOWARD: As someone who loves history and has grown fascinated with and attached to various historical figures, I'm wondering how you first became interested in Rebecca Boone.

PATRICIA L. HUDSON: In 1996, I happened upon Yale historian John Mack Faragher's biography of Daniel Boone. I took it home, and though Daniel was interesting, what really fascinated me were the glimpses Faragher provided of the Boone women. I wanted to know more about them, and that led to years of research, gathering the traces of them that remained in the historical record.

Patricia L. Hudson

JKH: *Traces* is a remarkable exercise in introspection; you put us fully in the minds of Rebecca, Jemima, and Susannah Boone. Yet it also has some exciting action sequences. I'm thinking here of the enthralling opening. What are the pleasures and challenges of writing both internal thought and action?

PLH: It's a bit like walking a tightrope—it's crucial to keep both elements balanced. Action provides momentum and keeps the story moving forward, but without sufficient interiority, characters don't come alive for your readers. Of course, the opposite is true, as well. Too much interiority can slow the story to a crawl. My goal for *Traces* was to make readers feel immersed in these women's thoughts and feelings, so that you felt as if you were moving through their eighteenth-century world right alongside them.

JKH: The historical details in this book are so rich. How did you accomplish the fine balance it takes to make it all accurate yet not putting too much research on the page?

PLH: My first career was as a university reference librarian, and my second was as a journalist, so research is something I enjoy. It's easy for me to get caught up in tracking down some obscure tidbit of information because my library degree trained me to keep searching until I found an answer. As a novelist, I had to continually remind myself to ignore the things that didn't specifically serve the novel. The image that comes to mind when I think about my research process is a layer cake. I used research to form the base layer—gathering and laying out all the known historical facts about Rebecca, Susannah and Jemima.

Once I knew where each of the three women would have been, geographically, at each point in their lives, as well as who they were interacting with at the time, I built story arcs for each of them, and only after that did I go back and add another layer of research—sort of like the frosting—putting in all the little details that help readers feel as if they've actually stepped back in time. At this final stage I went scene by scene to gauge whether my research was overpowering the story—assessing what needed to be cut, or in some cases, where details needed to be added. Of course, the process is a bit messier than I've just described, but a layer cake is a pretty serviceable analogy for how I handle research—it's the foundation and the frosting.

JKH: A major theme of the novel is reclaiming women's stories in history, which are often erased, dismissed, overlooked or forgotten. What were your major sources of documentation for the lives of the Boone women?

PLH: About that erasure—my parents took me to Colonial Williamsburg when I was eight, and though I was fascinated by the movie at the visitor's center that depicted the events that led up to the American Revolution, the women were barely visible; mostly they just waved goodbye to the men who went off to do all the daring deeds. So even at that young age, I recognized that the women's stories were missing.

Later, as a college history major, I became even more aware of how our country's primary historical records preserve History, not Herstory. For the most part, the women we know even a small bit about appear in the records in relation to a man—be that father, brother or husband. It's too late to recover most of these long forgotten women's stories, but writers of historical fiction can write at least some of the women back into history by gleaning what they can from the existing records, then adding both imagination and intuition to render their stories as realistically as possible.

Daniel became famous at the age of fifty when a land speculator named John Filson published the frontiersman's stories. Filson didn't even bother to record any of the Boone women's names. Most of the information we have about them was collected in the mid-nineteenth century by a man named Lyman Draper. He was obsessed with the pioneer generation, and wound up interviewing the few pioneers who were still alive at that time, as well as their children and grandchildren. His collection, which is housed at the Wisconsin Historical Society, is an indispensible resource for our knowledge of the frontier period. I did most of my research using the Draper Manuscripts, which were available on microfilm at the East Tennessee History Center. I also used both Faragher's biography, and a more recent biography of Boone by Robert Morgan. I consider Morgan's biography to be the best one available, because he grew up in western North Carolina and brings a poet's eye to the telling, as well as a bone-deep understanding of Appalachia.

JKH: Your novel gives us a much more critical eye on Daniel Boone than previous books have done, yet he is also not a villainous character. Talk about that decision.

PLH: When I first started my research, I really didn't want to like Daniel. Seriously, he left Rebecca on her own to farm and raise a cabin full of children; she birthed ten children, and the family adopted eight others who'd been orphaned. Despite the unspeakable workload such an enormous family created, Daniel felt entitled to disappear into the wilderness, sometimes for years at a time. He justified it by saying the fur trade was how he supported the family, and that's true up to a point, but it's pretty clear that many of his excursions were simply because of his love of wilderness. He was an explorer at heart.

Much of the time I wanted to grab Daniel by the shoulders and shake some sense into him for Rebecca's sake, but I also, rather reluctantly, found him to be extremely likable. He was, by all accounts, a kind man. He had a deep respect for the Native Americans, which was highly unusual for that time period. He managed to maintain both Cherokee and Shawnee friendships throughout his life. He was also endlessly resilient and inclined to make the best of whatever situation he found himself in. In his old age, he was the sort of grandfather who bounced the babies on his knee and told jokes to the older children. I wound up admiring him in spite of myself.

JKH: Much of Daniel Boone's story is either rooted in or connected to ideas and actions that we now view much more critically—colonialism, Manifest Destiny, the removal of Native peoples, etc. How did you reckon with that in approaching this novel? Did it add another layer of difficulty in writing the book?

PLH: Telling this story definitely presented challenges. The United States is only now beginning to seriously confront the ugliest parts of our history. While I believe it's long past due, it did create some difficulties for *Traces*. One of the first things my agent said when she saw the manuscript was, "You'll have to find sensitivity readers." My search for a Shawnee sensitivity reader is a saga all by itself.

We recognize now that the "wilderness" wasn't just empty space—it was home to many different native peoples who fought hard to keep it. As the settlers pushed westward, the idea of Manifest Destiny was woven into our country's birth story in an effort to absolve what was, in reality, a slow-rolling genocide.

While *Traces* is told through the eyes of three eighteenth-century white women, I took every possible opportunity within the novel to depict the Native American side of things. My research showed me that Jemima, like her father, didn't harbor ill will towards the Native Americans in spite of being kidnapped by them at one point in her life. I suspect when the women got the chance to know the people their own culture viewed as "other," they recognized that human beings of every race are alike, a complex mixture of both good and bad traits.

JKH: The process of fictionalizing historical figures is interesting, but it comes with some particular challenges. What are they?

PLH: One of the challenges I set for myself was to follow the historical record as closely as possible. What interested me was putting these women in the places and situations they actually experienced, and then doing my best to discern what they might have been thinking and feeling.

None of the three women were literate, so their voices have been lost. All that remains are the things others said about them, not what they might have said about themselves. Sticking as closely as possible to the way the actual events unfolded was my way of trying to honor the lives these women actually led.

That said, as a novelist, I occasionally had to shift the timing of an event, or combine several occurrences into a single scene to keep the novel from sprawling too much. For example, an incident I recount about Jemima at the

Cumberland River occurred the way I depict it, but it actually happened a couple years later. Because that event offered a window into Jemima's character, I needed to include it, but because I wasn't going to show the later journey along Boone's Trace, it was necessary to move it, time-wise.

When an historical novelist tinkers with history, I believe they should be able to articulate why any changes they've made were necessary.

JKH: One of the most interesting aspects of the Boone story is the way Rebecca was accused of having had an affair with her husband's brother, and you do a beautiful job of writing about that situation with complexity. The historical record is sparse on that relationship, but there were certainly rumors and gossip. Did you have to rely more on your own imagination for that subplot?

PLH: Every biography of Daniel highlights the rumors, so this story of adultery has been the main impression many readers have of Rebecca. I wanted people to know that all three of the Boone women were so much more than the rumors that have followed them down to the present. I researched the rumors as thoroughly as possible, and I while I don't want to spoil the novel by revealing whether I decided the rumors were true or not, it's clear the women lived with whispers and innuendo for most of their lives.

JKH: Did you visit any of the real locations, such as Fort Boonesborough, while researching the novel? If so, how did that change your perspective?

PLH: I felt it was critical to visit all the locations connected to the Boones, and that task was made a great deal easier by a wonderful guidebook by North Carolina author, Randell Jones, called *In the Footsteps of Daniel Boone*. It led me to so many sites, not just the famous ones like Boonesborough, but also house sites, many of which don't have historical markers. Traveling the back roads in the areas associated with the Boones, gave me a good idea of the terrain and geographical landmarks they would have known. There were a lot of locations all over Appalachia to visit because the family was perpetually on the move.

Standing beside the Kentucky River, on the grassy plain that was the original site of Fort Boonesborough, was invaluable for writing about the various battles that took place there. Although the terrain has changed to a degree, the ridgeline known as Hackberry Ridge remains, as do the bluffs on the far side of the river. It's haunting to stand on that patch of ground and think about the events that occurred there

In addition to Fort Boonesborough, there are a number of other outstanding living history sites that depict frontier life, such as Martin's Station in southwest Virginia, which was the final outpost of "civilization" before travellers passed through Cumberland Gap. The reenactors at Martin's Station, as well as several other living history sites, patiently answered my copious questions about daily life on the frontier.

JKH: What did you find to be the most interesting aspect of Rebecca Boone's life?

PLH: I think the fact that she managed, in the face of unimaginable hardships, to grow as a person and gain at least some level of agency over her own life. I came to that conclusion by comparing two descriptions of her that miraculously have survived. The earliest description of Rebecca was from a journal entry made by a Moravian minister who visited the Boone cabin in North Carolina. "She is by nature a quiet soul, and of few words..." he wrote. "She told me of her trouble, and of the frequent distress and fear in her heart." Daniel wasn't yet famous, so this missionary viewed Rebecca as just another backcountry housewife.

Another vignette of Rebecca that has survived tells us that, years later, she was brave enough to shame an entire fort of men who she deemed were paying insufficient attention to protecting the women and children. Those two views of her, one uncertain and fearful, the other courageous and decisive, shaped my portrayal of her.

JKH: What's the best thing you learned about yourself—as a person and/or as a writer—while writing this novel?

PLH: This lengthy journey, from original idea to actually holding the book in my hand, taught me how to persevere through the sort of self-doubt that plagues most writers. I proved to myself that a long-time journalist could learn the craft of fiction, and I discovered that networking with other writers is critical when pursuing one's dream of publication. Most of all, I'm proud to have helped Rebecca and her girls step out from behind Daniel's shadow. ■

REBORN

after the first monsoon showers,
the drain gushes forth in frothy
abundance, its waters a trampoline
for jumping tadpoles and vain dragon-
flies that hover inches above, flapping
their wings thirty times per second,
and of course, the algae hieroglyphs
lining the parapet walls on either side
of the drain, still as undeciphered—
for much is lost in translation, even
of silence, imposing and green and
already repeated a million million times
before we arrived here.

FAIZ AHMAD

SUNSET PHOTOGRAPHERS

Somewhere between tobacco & kerosene
the lake at sunset stretched from amber to
amber, banked by the sterile, cracked clay
that laid bare the earth's geriatric austerities
beneath the suspended shape of an air-mass
—draconian and, as if it were a precondition,
vulnerable—as the heated glass of a burning
oil lamp and the raptors glide in, buzzing like
an orchestra of moths, soaring and encircling,
scavengers biding their flames, and at the far
edge by the withering marsh grasses, the faint
silhouette of two lone, human figures, alert &
desperate with their DSLRs, salvaging what
they can from this immense spectacle of all
consuming fire: the penultimate hue of things,
the ever-elusive number of birds—odd/even.

FAIZ AHMAD

THE OLD TELEPHONE POLE

having played your part
in humanity's victory
           over geography

ferried clandestine vibrations
back and forth between
           the secret lips of
           long distance lovers

to mother's imagination
you supplied the raw materials
           the voice of her son
           in another state

your duties you carried out
most commendably

but look at you now
ten-feet tall in the post-Newtonian
universe

so blaringly defunct
so pitiably out of pitch
           creepers and rust bless
           your irrelevance

in the age of automation
where you stand,
marvellously unemployed

by men as much as by angels

FAIZ AHMAD

AFTER SPINOZA

We are the sparse population
dotting the evening landscape.

The dense cold air hunched
around us, a Euclidean beast.

The birds are shrinking chalk points
in the grey slate of the sky,
and the dark sea has been chained
into quiet shapeliness.

Upon the coffee table,
the solitary teacup rests with a geometrical
certainty between the two of us.

In the overpowering stillness
        of our earth,
to exchange *promises* seemed to
be the only natural response,
our little axiom,
our human way of rhyming
        with the stable arrangement of things.

A shuffle of steps
as we start to rise & walk towards
the café door, not thinking of that teacup
        round and magisterial
like a pulsating orb,

before it was whisked away into oblivion,
by the waiter's
> sleight of hands.

FAIZ AHMAD

CHECKING OUT

SARAH LADD

I start when I see the skinny little boxes of orange Tic Tacs next to the green gum packages and ChapSticks. I half expect Grannie to lean past me in the checkout line and scoop them all onto the belt, her eyes grinning at me from behind small, round glasses.

I shiver the memory away. She's gone.

While I wait for the cashier, I flip my credit card between my fingers, recalling how that $20 bill felt the last time I saw Grannie alive. I'd come to visit her in a Paducah, Kentucky hospital bed. Her legs were swollen and purple with the failed kidneys, and I had come to visit after work, just for a minute, in my greasy McDonald's uniform that never quite smelled clean, even when it was.

My cheeses, fruits, and meats are all stacked and still on the Kroger conveyor belt as my bored eyes drift, and then my mind.

■ ■ ■

The very last time I saw my Grannie alive, she gave me twenty bucks for a case of the orange Tic Tacs I used to like so much. I haven't eaten them since then, and it's been nigh on eight years. Any time I see them, I also expect to see her long slender fingers, outstretched toward me. You know what I mean to say, right? How missing someone can taste like candy, so much so that you can't bring yourself to spoil the memories, to remind your tongue of tang.

Miss Sarah E she breathed at me as I entered her hospital room, adjusting her weight on the bed to look more composed, and smiling from thin crimson lips.

She'd called me that for as long as I could remember. I can't even recall how that got started, but it set me apart among my many brothers and sisters. She called all of them by just their name. But me? I was special to her. Listen to me, clinging to that all these years later, trying to convince myself more than you.

She'd been in and out of doctor's offices my whole life, so seeing her in the hospital seemed like any other normal day. Except this time, her normally white legs were almost black and infected and oozing. Once I saw them, I couldn't look away for many seconds, and she didn't bother to try and cover them. Silence between us, briefly.

I wasn't there long, standing stiff at the foot of her bed, close enough to the door to make a quick exit, when she reached into her big floral cloth purse, pulled out her billfold and handed me a stiff twenty-dollar bill.

We did our normal dance. The *Oh Grannie I could never take that, you don't have to do that* and her reply, in a high-pitched voice that screamed offense: *I know that, dear, I want to. Take it and buy yourself some orange Tic Tacs.* Then the awkward hug over her bed, just too low for my bend to be natural.

I wish there was a way to know when you're seeing someone for the very last time.

I should have studied harder the twist in her tiny lips, the blankness in those greying eyes. I shouldn't have laughed off why she would give me $20 for Tic Tacs when they didn't even cost five. There are lots of things I should have done, and chief of all is this: I should have stayed in that little sterile room longer. I said something about being tired from work and wanting to get home. I did not say it was awkward to be here, that the pain of seeing her weak was too much for me, that I selfishly didn't want to remember her like this. I did not take time to wonder how she felt beyond the pain, if she felt alone.

■ ■ ■

Grannie first went to the hospital the Monday before Thanksgiving, 2015. She didn't want to go, Momma tells me. She somehow knew if she left her little house on Front Street, she would never see it again. A woman's intuition, perhaps?

Her kidneys were shutting down. What was there to do? Nothing. Momma went over to the house several times every day to lift her from the floor after she fell. She couldn't get in and out of bed.

The hospital called Momma on Thanksgiving. Grannie's oxygen had dropped, and she had to go into intensive care. She was so confused, far too young to be that confused. And then there she was, sent off to inpatient rehab, with me far too scared to visit. I imagined all the people there staring at me with their blank faces, erased of all recognition by horrible diseases.

If I had known she had only a month to live, maybe I would have braved it. But I couldn't have known, right? She was just seventy-one. And she was *my* grandmother. Other people's grandmothers could die, but not mine.

Momma called me on January 2nd, wailing, to tell me Grannie was forever gone. I was kneeling on my red couch inside the bug-infested apartment in Mayfield, Kentucky that I could afford, and thus called home. I don't remember how she

> *I did not cry then. In fact, the news barely moved me. I thought in that moment something must be terribly wrong with me.*

told me. I remember only that she was sobbing and suddenly the world felt colder, empty of fudge and homemade potato candy at Christmas, void of Friday nights at Grannie's house, eating pizza together and watching old western shows like *Bonanza* and *Have Gun, Will Travel*.

I did not cry then. In fact, the news barely moved me. I thought in that moment something must be terribly wrong with me. How could I be so selfish to not visit, so cold not to cry? It took me years to cry for her, and even longer to visit her grave. For that, too, *I am sorry.*

■ ■ ■

Before I left home at nineteen, I was Grannie's companion for years. She lived just five minutes from the family farm, having moved from Tennessee to be closer to us.

Because of her many health challenges, she needed to make the forty-five-minute trip to Paducah regularly for doctor's appointments. My older sister, Ruth, and I piled in the blue Chevy that smelled like Grannie's Elizabeth Taylor perfume and we jostled down old rural roads toward the city. Ruth drove and I sat in the back beside Grannie's folded walker, holding my breath for long moments at a time to ward off that sharp, old-smelling perfume that attacked my head with migraines and my eyes with throbs.

We made whole days of those trips. First up was Grannie's doctor appointment. In 1996, when I was just two years old and Grannie still lived just north of Memphis, she was on her way to visit us when someone ran a red light and crashed into her, crushing her leg. This happened somewhere along the road between Dyersburg and Covington, Momma says. For months Grannie lingered in Memphis rehab, not able to bear weight and stand.

When her father, my great-grandaddy who lived on the farm with us, died that December, she couldn't come. After that, she walked with a walker and leg brace. So, we went to the podiatrists' offices all the time so they could look at her feet. Sometimes, they had to shave off hard chunks of what she said was crushed bone, working its way out of her body. It's amazing, how much bone a human body has. It just kept coming.

After the awful medical business was over, we'd go to lunch, on Grannie's dime. We oscillated from Cracker Barrel and the cold crunchy chicken salads to Bob Evans and the three-cheese burger to Olive Garden and the lasagna followed by small after-lunch mints. Grannie folded her hands together over her belly or on the table and flirted with all the young male waiters.

They blushed, embarrassed by her attention. When they hurried away, she giggled and giggled, her eyes lit like glass on a beach.

After lunch it was off to Sam's Club, where we walked up and down aisles for hours. Grannie piled into her buggy all sorts of things she thought I would love—a pair of furry purple boots, a family sized pack of M&Ms, and scarves. Always, too, she would find a jumbo pack of orange Tic Tacs. I tried to hoard and save them because my parents didn't buy candy, and it was a rare treat. But I never could. Instead, I stuffed my mouth full and sucked on the cream coating, then the sugar and tang.

■ ■ ■

Right after Grannie's death I went with my mother to the funeral home in Bardwell to pick out the casket I would later carry, alongside my sisters. It's weird, isn't it? To pick a color and a price tag to be someone's forever home, their last bed. I stared at the catalog while my mother sat still and mute beside me. The funeral director looked too serious to honor someone who laughed as much as Grannie. I shifted in my chair before him.

I said I thought Grannie would like the blue one. I don't know why I said it. Maybe because Grannie, a few years prior while in her late sixties, had received a recruitment pamphlet from the United States Marine Corps. She laughed and cackled over it for weeks, showing everyone how she was still wanted by her country. She wondered aloud how she'd look in dress blue slacks. *So dignified,* I told her, slapping my thigh and snorting with laughter. That casket's shade looked like the dress blue slacks. I chuckled softly, then cleared my throat. It wasn't appropriate to laugh there.

■ ■ ■

91

My first and only time carrying a casket was for Grannie. I don't even know why it was important to me. My family, notoriously patriarchal, didn't look to her as being a family matriarch. But her death crushed my mother and spread grief among us like dust you can't catch with a broom. My sisters and I decided to carry Grannie from the funeral home to the hearse, a family first, our desperate attempt to hug her a final time.

The six of us, heeled and in black, stumbled under her despite being braced for the weight. I'm not sure what I expected, but certainly not the weight that made me feel the weakest I've ever felt. My arms shook. I thought embalming made a person lighter.

I could feel everyone's eyes on us as we struggled. I thought for a few seconds that the points of my dress shoes would pierce through the floor. Or crush my ankle. My face reddened with the strain and shame of it all.

My brothers and the male funeral home staff rushed beside my sisters and me, lifting Grannie. My sisters and I, after only making it fifteen feet or so, stepped out from under her and let the trained staff finish the job. I wanted to look into my sisters' eyes, one by one, to see if they were as embarrassed as I. But the floor pulled at my head, and I could only look down.

I felt in that moment and for these years since that I failed her, a horrible act of betrayal. I followed the men and the coffin to the hearse, and I watched them shove her with ease into the blackness. My throat hurt.

■ ■ ■

The week after Grannie died, I thought I saw her in the Walmart near my apartment, her hips swinging wide with her signature limp behind a creaking old buggy. I stopped in the baking aisle and hurried after her, leaving my buggy unattended. People stared at me, a crazy young woman whose red cheeks held in the tears I wouldn't let to my eyes. I searched for her, aisle after aisle, and she was gone. Not even her scent trailed her.

When I sniffed at the air, no Elizabeth Taylor, only cocoa powder and syrup. The makings of candy.

■ ■ ■

Just this? the cashier pulls at my attention.

I look around. It's just me here now, alone, in the checkout line. The woman who was purchasing the trimmings of a BBQ seconds ago has disappeared. I sniff at the air subconsciously from behind my COVID-era mask. No whiffs of that awful Elizabeth Taylor perfume Grannie used to drench herself in, giving me throbbing migraines and blurred eyeballs. I don't miss the migraines, just what they meant: that she used to be here. The bread loaf in my hands is weightless compared to her coffin, but I find my fingers are gripping it and my feet braced for heavy lifting.

My mouth waters as I look from the cashier to the orange Tic Tacs, but I don't reach for them. I can't eat them anymore. I worry they won't taste how I remember them at all. Or that I will somehow dishonor her by eating them now, like a failed attempt at time travel, I will go back to that sweet-sour taste, and she will still be gone.

Just this. ■

MY BLUEBIRD

there's a bluebird in my heart   driven by dearth
the poor earth so winter-marred   my mother's voice
at my throat   I'll give you something   to cry about

there's a bluebird in my heart   it is true
a little weather-worn   feathers captured a piece of sky
harried by storm so long   and we sleep together like that

there's a bluebird in my heart that   said oh,
I was looking for you   I just came to tell you   facts,
valuable information, secret reports   and soft she sighed

there's a bluebird in my heart   in the snow with an axe
a voice that could broom sorrow   carries reprimand and care
swats me as I carry   seeking   finding no way out

there's a bluebird in my heart that found interment there
when everybody's asleep   shouts joy to nobody   atonement
   don't be sad   don't be sad   don't be sad   don't be sad

JOSH NICOLAISEN

This poem is a cento composed from Katherine Lee Bates's "The First Bluebirds," Charles Bukowski's "The Bluebird," Emily Dickinson's "The Bluebird," Robert Frost's "The Last Word of a Bluebird," Herman Melville's "The Blue-Bird," Joyce Peseroff's "Bluebird," and Carl Sandburg's "Bluebird, What Do You Feed On."

SHELBY

You left for San Francisco with your friends,
and I am here—it's not even lunch yet—
wandering through my new neighborhood,

the houses like chrysanthemums, so many
colors, and the blocks speckled sometimes
with blight. I look in one yard, shaded,

tin sculptures of flowers gaudy, all the petals
circular like clocks, and I forgot to tell you
that I looked up your name, which comes

from Old English, something like "dweller
of the willow place." I once saw a Mississippi
Kite slated on a willow, unperturbed

by a mockingbird's churr, screeches operatic
in the sprigs. The northern mockingbird,
I think, means something like "many-tongued

thrush," and this one dashes to the weeds
impasto on the chain-link fence. If I describe
things like this, will you want to come home?

I keep thinking about Walter Inglis Anderson
climbing down tied bed sheets, dangling beneath
some institution's window as he muraled the wall—

birds in flight—with a bar of Ivory soap.
He loved pelicans, as you do, and rowed
to Horn Island, painting them and other

scenes, sometimes his only company a possum.
I would drive you to Ocean Springs right now,
if I could, because I am recalling his mural

at this community center, pelicans aloft near
the window, their bills cerulean and blood orange,
bodies lavender, and the totipalmate feet teal,

or like teal, all of this not decorative but felt.
You would say that the red-orbed eyes
aren't alive enough, and you'd be right,

though you're not here, and aren't these
ornithological changes a clearer vision,
because how many photographs and

paintings have we passed over, their rendering
so precise they disappear—do you know
what I mean? I can't forget the unreal floral

plumage. I can't forget the apricot star-leafed
tree, sinuous bark, the hills or clouds, the dreamy
fauna from a man in love with his loneliness.

But I'm not in love like that.
It was just this morning, the very early morning,
when we said goodbye, the blue touch of your hands.

BURNSIDE SOLEIL

JEREMY

We woke on the wooden floor,
and in the corner of the room,
cups of rain—your roof leaking.

Your window framed moss on the oak,
where two hawks landed, ruddy-barred
chests, and we watched and had nowhere

to be, and this morning a single hawk,
young, darker feathers, hushed the electric-
like hum of cicadas in the pine.

It's been twenty years, and the rain
still cools the September air, for now.
Those cups—plastic carnival throws—

you'd fill with flowers, mums, purple
and bronze, all plucked from the neighbor's
garden where she kept the dog leashed.

And the ceiling mold was like a watercolor
black sea. You used to like things like that,
mushrooms bracketing a snag.

We couldn't really know each other now.
There are stories maybe, like this evening
when two white egrets—forget symbols—

plumed in the median, and then one flying
to the bayou, the other nearly into my car.
I pulled over, wondering if the bird

had noticed me. It landed in the shells
spined along the shore and then vanished
by the overpass. Scales seemed to drift

from the oak branches—there were so many,
these lace bugs. And was it wrens darting
tree to tree? Childhood is deciduous.

If only we could have seen this before
the summer you left—these wrens pitched
after lace bugs, this feast of golden scales.

BURNSIDE SOLEIL

THE JAR
& THE BEETLE
(& THE RHINOCEROS)

RICHARD HAGUE

Part One

Not long ago, I asked my wife Pam Korte, a teacher of ceramics and a professional potter for the last forty-five years or so, what she thought about the notion of "paying attention." I wasn't looking for something abstract, but for concrete specifics. Paying attention to what? Paying attention when? Why? For what purposes? Over breakfast she delivered an impromptu lecture-reflection based on her daily morning walk of our nosy, yappy, needy, mulch-gobbling rescue dog Quinn. She said that despite being distracted by the beast's herky-jerky lurching and tugging, "I look at the same things every morning, because I usually take the same walk. I'm looking for things like weight, and balance, and distribution of space."

I pressed for even more examples. Our neighborhood is an old one, having first been settled sometime before 1809, and there are lots of big trees, shrubs, old gardens, so there's a lot to look at. "How a branch weighs down with water in front of Mr. Nash's old house, for example," she said. "How a weedstalk bends, in the garden next to the driveway, how a stem, at a node, swells and then narrows again. That kind of thing." That was her take on what she called "weight."

"So what do you mean by 'balance'?" I asked.

"Well, that involves how something keeps itself upright or not. Lots of flowers have big heads on really skinny stems: cleomes, zinnias, sunflowers. How do they do that? I'm interested in whether they remain upright or not, I'm interested in whether the flowers follow the sun or not."

And what about "distribution of space"?

She said, "All the edges of flowers have some sort of division of space at their ends. Some are more regular than others. Some are smooth, some are notched, or divided. There are even names for these variations. I have flower books that describe them. So not only the flower petals and leaves themselves, but the negative space between them; I pay attention to that as much as everything else."

"Why?" I asked.

She said, "I'm trying to punctuate my pots"—she actually used that word *punctuate*, as if pots could be a kind of writing—"with them, and I'm trying to bring spaces like that to my writing, too. Sometimes, after flowing along for a while in a paragraph, I just stop a sentence, dead. Wham. Period. For effect." (For three years, my wife has been studying writing, memoir in particular, with the Weatherford Award-winning poet, writer, and teacher Pauletta Hansel. And many years ago, Pam and I did a joint workshop at the Kentucky Country Day School in Louisville in which we tried to blend our conversation about pottery and poetry—words which, by the way, share all the same letters—to make points about art in general with the students.)

Then as now, it has become clear that Pam and I have developed, almost unconsciously, a kind of aesthetic vocabulary for what we do: hers is a floral lexicon, describing various forms of attractive flow and regularity in plants that eventually inform her pots. She had a show a few years back in which every piece was influenced by flower forms; later, she curated a show called *Biophilia*, which included pottery, printmaking, letterpress printing, and poetry about the natural world. She pointed out that my take on insects was from a quite different perspective—unlike flowers, insects are almost all bilaterally symmetrical, with their variation of form and pattern following the rules of equal balance very closely. Left and right are mirror images, as clearly opposed and balanced as top and bottom—dorsal and ventral, to use the entymological terms. Her pots are radial, literally—being mostly thrown on a wheel, rather than being hand-built. My insects are spiny, edgy, branchy, jagged, horny, winged, antlered—but not so much radial. A single monster Class of animals, Insecta, of astonishing diversity of size and form, but all of the same basic architecture. *E Pluribus Unum.*

■ ■ ■

Take Two

Imagine a young person at a zoo. Before her, separated by a little moat, is a collection of, say, miraculous and unbelievable mini-rhinoceroses, fairy pachyderms. There are all sorts of ins and outs to any rhinoceros, all sorts of plates and folds and textures and bulgings and saggings and hornings-out then suddenly, around the eyes, and in the interior of the ears, infoldings, indentations. See, for example, Albrecht Durer's woodcut of a rhinoceros. The animal is an entire world in itself; its topography, if you will, is as varied as any earth's. It is pocked and bossed and bulged with craters, caldera, layered with plates, edged with spikes and horns and splinters and hairs; its head-horn is crocketted with fractal protuberances growing out of iterations of overlapping scales, its neck-horn a little cone of concentrics. Its forelegs wear sleeves of pocked leather stamped with a hundred Saturns. The beast seems composed of continents, of all geology.

So this girl, wanting to get as close a look as possible at these detailed but undersized marvels, leans over the moat, stretching as far as is possible without losing her footing and tipping over: attentive, she is doing everything she can physically to get closer. She is literally enacting the etymology of the word "attention." It comes from two Latin roots which translate literally as "to stretch toward." Our artistic understanding of paying attention is not only that physical stretch, but in terms of the arts, the stretching of the consciousness and intuition and craft as close to the object as is possible. Paying attention is just that: expending energy in perceiving up close. (I first wrote, "seeing up close," but I realized that it is not only the visual that we pay attention to, but the aural and the tactile and the olfactoral. This is why customers in my wife's studio so often touch or pick up her work, or why careful shoppers smell the cantaloupe before paying for it, or why the symphony-goer leans slightly forward in her seat, to catch all the subtleties of the music.)

■ ■ ■

Take Three

Photography and cinema: two arts which require precise observation and careful framing of what is being paid attention to. One of the two great early Russian filmmakers, a contemporary of Sergei Eisenstein, was a man carrying the heavy, gravity-laden name of V. I. Pudovkin. (I love the bristly, fence-like look of the letters of his name: imagine printing it carefully and boldly out: many sharp uprights, several Vs, pointed and keen-edged as shivs, and that shin-kicking K: that'll get your attention.) Pudovkin wrote, "To show something as everyone else has seen it, is to accomplish nothing." This seems to me to be the challenge any creative writer faces: to find some way of seeing, to find an angle of attention, that refreshes and renews the vision, rather than merely confirms it. Paying attention is what reveals the uncommon in the common, the surprising in the routine. It is the stuff of epiphanies.

■ ■ ■

Take Four

Consider the beetle.
It is the most numerous and various family of living things on the planet; estimates of the number of species comprising

Coleoptera range from 250,000 to over a million. It is a fact (and a clue to our lack of attention or a confirmation of the infinite variety of nature) that hundreds of thousands of species remain undiscovered.

The beetle ranges in size from almost microscopic to the aptly named Goliath beetle, six-inches long and as heavy as a shoe. (One writer reports that it sounds like a small plane approaching as it flies through the jungle.) Beetles occupy practically every ecological niche, including the surface of the ocean (there are aquatic species in and under fresh water).

The beetle is tough and beautiful, with an often bejeweled exoskeleton protecting it from being pierced, crushed, or desiccated. It may be striped, spotted, cross-hatched, iridescent, bossed, indented; it may be blue, aureate, deep purple, topaz; it may be boxishly square, sinuously elongated, roughly crenellated, horned, antlered, or smooth and black as polished jet. It has many parts, all connected to one another in the intricate ways of the arthropod.

It requires of those who would study it a specialized and exotic vocabulary: *dorsal, ventral, plastron, thorax, elytra, mandible.*

Its origins are prehistoric. Its future, as best we can determine—even in this Anthropocene Age of climate change and global warming, of mass extinctions and precipitous plunges of local populations—is probably assured.

It can fly.

■ ■ ■

Now consider the poem.

It is the most varied of literary genres and is constantly in flux, limited in its form and style only by the inventiveness of nature as channeled by the poet's imagination. Thousands of possible formal and aural and visual variations of poetry remain undiscovered and untried.

The poem ranges in size from the one-liner (the monostich) to the book-length (or multi-volume) epic. Its subject matter is unbounded; there are fabulous poems about God (*Paradise Lost,* for example, or *The Book of Job*) and fabulous poems about dung (Maxine Kumin's "The Excrement Poem").

It is, when well-made, something like an organism or something like a particularly fine machine; we can perceive the connection of its parts, each reciprocating with the other (or deliberately and purposefully not), and we can admire and learn from what has been called the successful poem's "cohabition of images." We can see and hear that it is "language listening to itself."

If we would take its study and practice seriously, we would learn its special vocabulary: *anaphora, epiphora, cadence, anapest, litotes, synechdoche, quatrain.*

Poetry is probably the most ancient verbal art, and its current renewal and widening popularity and re-evolution into a performance art is exciting and richly arguable.

A good poem flies; it raises us up on what Keats called the "viewless wings of poesy."

■ ■ ■

As a boy, perhaps the most important work I did as a future poet was to collect and study beetles. The habits of observing, classifying, mounting, and displaying my collection were the habits of the poet: concentration, naming the things of the world, the willingness to do something out of the ordinary, perseverance, the transformation of the unknown into the known, the slow adventure of moving from uncertainty to knowledge.

Beetles did not often come to me; I had to search them out. I had to learn their habits and their habitats, as well to master effective collecting techniques. Most of all, I had to acknowledge mystery; the lives of beetles took place almost entirely invisibly, so close to, and yet so distantly from my human world that I still can call up my original astonishment at how lively life is, how full and various, outside the human sphere. It is an awakening to the nature of things, and to a broader understanding of our place in Creation.

James Baldwin said, "Let's face it, the job of the writer is to notice things other people are too busy to notice." And Mary Oliver said, "To pay attention, this is our endless and proper work." Exactly. The poets I admire have, every one of them, accomplished some notable and unusual noticing. One of my poetic ancestors, Gerard Manley Hopkins, caught the detail, variety, and wild intensity of Creation in poems like "Pied Beauty."

> Glory be to God for dappled things—
> For skies of couple-colour as a brinded cow;
> For rose-moles all in stipple upon trout that swim;
> Fresh-firecoal chestnut-falls; finches' wings;
> Landscape plotted and pieced—fold, fallow, and plough;
> And áll trádes, their gear and tackle and trim.

Years ago, Pauletta Hansel kept a courageous months-long vigil with a dying man, Terrence Flanigan, helping to clean and feed him, watching him as he slept, observing his body and spirit in their sad decline in her poem "And Then":

> What's lost first
> after his body, sent to be ashes
> weeks ago?

Will you lose the bitter smell of him,
or the press of his bones
against your own,
or the crow of his laugh
shot across the room?

Even when it might be painful, even when it might remind us of loss, we keep our eyes wide open. The act of poetry, Robert Waldron says, is an act of "acute attention."

■ ■ ■

Take Five

A blazon is a form of poetry whose purpose is to list and praise the various qualities of the beloved. Shakespeare's "My mistress' eyes are nothing like the sun" is a playful example of a blazon in reverse, listing and describing each of the beloved's physical attributes—her hair, her breath, her skin, her gait, but refusing to subscribe to the Petrarchan conventions of beauty that prevailed in his day. "To show something as everyone else has shown it is to accomplish nothing." So Shakepeare's is a kind of anti-blazon, actually—its rejection of conventions still a useful strategy for poets today. Let me offer humbly a personal example of making a poem by reversing conventional ways of seeing something common, even cliched in a cutesy sort of way, in this age of You Tube cat videos.

"House Cats." (I pause here for you to call up the usual visions of cutesy-wootsy furballs tangling with a piece of string on the kitchen floor, or such-like over-sweet visual bon-bons.) Now, here goes with avoiding showing something as everyone else has seen it:

Hatched from the blackest eggs of night,
asquawl on the stones of the suburbs,
they live to sneak beyond porch lights
toward the delicate warblings of wrens
dreaming in innocent shrubs.
Expert stalkers of the beautiful small—
shrew, field mouse, mantis—
they hunt merely to maul
with a rapid and finicky disgust.
Regularly, they eat their own hair.

Now will they answer to a name.
They want to be mysterious,
like Egypt,
who, to ride herself of their plague,
entombed them with her dead.
They want to be anonymous,
and to steal, like government spies or assassins,
through darkness forever,
silent,
sharpening their clever knives.

■ ■ ■

So back to the blazon. Any blazon arises from a careful attention not only to the most obvious, but also the subtlest qualities of the observed. "If hairs be wires, then black wires grow upon her head." Petrarch, establishing the conventions of Renaissance female beauty, described his beloved's tresses as golden wires. (Think Botticelli.) But Shakespeare's line rejects the conventional, offers us not the ideal, but the real.

If you please, walk mentally, imaginatively with me through this exercise: Look at an object hard and long. It may be something relatively simple like a wooden spoon or an antler or a shoe. Or it may be something intricate and complex, like a painting, a building, the body of your husband or wife or sleeping infant—or a beetle. Try to discover the "rules" of the thing, the governing rhythms or patterns of it. Find a way of saying those rules and patterns in ways that move away from the conventional, the trite, the clichéd. Try to see in this thing its extraordinary and lovely strangeness. Allow yourself to be surprised, both by the thing you are looking at, and by the language that arises as you labor playfully and seriously to express it. Write a blazon that lists, praises, describes various aspects of its beauty.

Wind Blazon

Its Touch

Its hand that
soared
the Alps, sailed the
glacier, stroked
the deep
Atlantic, rests
a moment,
warm now,
in her hair.

Its Hidden Parts

In some distant
cave of ice

it first dresses
itself.
It comes howling
out, Empress,
sabled in clouds.
All bows
as it
passes.

Its Voice

Sometimes wind
turns
to address us.
It gathers thunder
from far off
and drops it
mumbling
at our windows.

Its Body

Is like water flowing
over the grass,
or mist
with all the color
subtracted.
Hymns
rising between
leaves.

Its Delicacy

It suddenly lives
on the river,
a swash
like shoaling minnows

then
gone

Its Strength

In it the house collapses.
The fire rages.
The waterspout moans
like a diesel.

Its Delicacy

At night
in late Fall,
all the leaves down,
moon eyeing the sky,
wind lifts and carries
the last cricket's song
across ten acres
of woods.

Its Face

Is always
looking

back
toward trees
it has passed
through,
having shaken
itself free
from
small
branches.

Goodbye,
it whispers,

sayonara.

 I am very much an advocate of cross-training for writers, so I would say to prose writers too that the practice of attention affords novelists and essayists and biographers alike as many benefits as it does the poets I have mainly addressed. Stephen Jay Gould, science writer extraordinaire, explainer of everything from evolution to why so-called intelligence testing is not to be trusted, exclaims, "Nothing matches the holiness and fascination of accurate and intricate detail."
 We touch that holiness by paying attention. We create that fascination by studying closely and reporting and recreating with verve and freshness and accuracy the things of the world. We get what we pay for in paying attention: in this case, our writing, in all its pulsing detail and all its earned loveliness.
 I used to think it was just a dumb joke.
 But now I think I'm starting to see.
 He's telling us how it happens. ■

WHITMAN SPENT A SUMMER WRESTLING TREES

Timber Creek, Laurel Springs, New Jersey, 1876

I guess he did it
to show those trees who the boss was.
No...he considered them
equals, of course. Friends, even.
Walt Whitman did it for love.
For all of us. For American letters.
He did it for poetry. Turned experience
into art. Gave yet
more life to nature.
Whitman made the trees
speak. Or emote, at least.
Actually it was mainly for physical therapy.
After his second stroke, he was mostly paralyzed
and did it to regain his range of motion.
He also wrestled Harry Stafford
(the lucky son of his hosts) quite a bit that summer.
Trees! *Nature's gymnasia,* Whitman called them.
He'd had to press pause on his
perpetual stroll of the City, find the remote
spot with the most young beeches,
and get busy. He would exercise awhile,
bending a sapling, pushing and pulling, feeling
its young oaken virtue (or sycamore,
or hickory; even holly, now and then) course through him
and out of him in song. Next thing you know:
Timeless verse. *Specimen Days.* Prose
on dumb eloquence and silent strength,
imperturbability and *real being,* and we

thought they were just trees.
Just trees! Could they be
still standing, stronger
from their sessions with the poet?
If so I'd like to hear them sing. Let them
bend my ear for days and days.
Those trees and all
they've felt and seen!
Other than the boots and hat,
it's been reported Whitman grappled naked.

JEFF TIGCHELAAR

I THINK THEY CALL THIS *HERO WORSHIP*

The squirrel runs up and down the oak, the birch, the maple,
clips the flexible fresh growth—leaves gentle and pliant
as eyelids—and licks and fingers them into the new nest.
Sometimes he drops one and it curls and banks.
I have also quit things for unaccountable reasons, abandoned

the house I meant to be our first place, the dog I meant to be
our first dog. I want to go crashing through something,
not a window like a savior but undergrowth, waist-high fresh water,
the dream you have that makes you wake and clutch my thigh.
Let me believe I know what to cast and cast away, what to chuck
like a stone at a squirrel who pillages and says, *thanks for nothing.*

ASHLEY DANIELLE RYLE

CONSIDER ALL POSSIBLE ETYMOLOGIES OF CHARM IN *SOUTHERN CHARM*

Nuthatch is one of my favorite birds, his body a hilt-less dagger or the almond shape
of a wide but closing wound. I know he's a male because he swifts
to the fatpack of suet and inserts his beak with a certain practice and flings himself

back to the oak trunk, to the other nuthatch, and he slips her his tongue
like she's helpless and pink with being born, though she isn't,
which is common to most species. I think they call it white-knighting.

At our house on the cliff edge paths snake down to rockfall and foxtrot
and the bright water burps all afternoon with city people on freshly unwintered boats,
where, despite the warnings, the Louisville lawyers' wives rarely wear lifejackets.

I can't blame them. Sometimes I walk around naked when there's no call for it.

It's hard to unlearn that a man's gentleness might mean he cares a damn.

ASHLEY DANIELLE RYLE

WILDWOOD DRIVE

NANCY LUANA WILKES

Mrs. Smith's black hair was teased to heights that appeared unsafe, and her red lipstick suggested that she was not much good at coloring. But it was the first words she spoke that made me know that third grade at my new school was going to be a challenge.

"Good morning, class." She smiled big, and most of the red lipstick smiled with her. "I'd like to begin by going around the room and having you introduce yourselves. Tell me your name and your parents' names and what your father does for a living."

I stopped drawing tulips in the margins of my new notebook paper.

What my father does for a living?

My father didn't work. He lived with his regular-law wife or whatever she was called, and they drank beer and fished, and he went to jail sometimes for punching her. In the five years since Mom made him leave, I'd probably only seen him three times. My thoughts tumbled like the letters and numbers in the Bingo machine. Mailman. Phone man. Policeman. My stomach began to cramp as the question crept closer.

It was Mary's turn to answer. She was in the desk in front of me.

"My name is Mary Mason. My Mom's name is Dorris, and my father's name is Mr. Mason. He works for Sears," she said. She sat up taller in her desk. "Sometimes he flies on airplanes."

"Thank you, Mary," Mrs. Smith said. "What in the world would we do without Sears?"

I glanced up and acted surprised that it was my turn. "My name is Nancy Wilkes," I began. "My mom's name is Ruby, and my father's name is Jimmy—Ruby Wilkes and Jimmy Wilkes."

I tried to will the question to be over, will my answer to be deemed sufficient for a passing grade.

"And what does your father do?" Mrs. Smith asked.

The moment was awkward not only for me but for my classmates as well, some of whom were also my neighbors. They were kids who worried about being chosen last in kickball, not what my father did for a living. Some looked at the floor, others out the window. When the moment went on longer than any of us could stand, my friend Mike tried to help us out. "Mrs. Smith, Nancy doesn't have a father."

"I do too!" I yelled. "Yes, I do!"

Some kid in the back who I did not know said, "Oh, yeah, then tell the teacher what he does for work."

I searched the pencil holder on the top of my desk. I searched Mike's apologetic eyes, and for the rest of my life I would wonder where my next words came from.

"My father is an astronaut. That's why he's gone a lot."

Neil Armstrong had walked on the moon just one month earlier, and the world had stood still, holding its breath. Just like there had been perfect silence around the world as his foot touched the moon, there was now perfect silence in my third-grade classroom. Mrs. Smith pursed her badly painted lips together, and I am pretty sure in that moment she made the decision to never ask her class this question again. I knew that my classmates—the ones whose parents gave me rides to school when it was raining, the ones whose phone numbers stayed on a pad in the kitchen drawer so I could call them if I needed someone when Mom was at work—they would tell their parents what I'd said. Their parents would kindly explain to them the situation, and that would simply be the end of it. So, I continued.

"Sometimes he has to go places on the rockets. Places other people don't know about yet. He's not the main astronaut, though."

I twisted in my desk and looked to the back of the room inviting the boy there to challenge me. I noticed that he had a fat face and too many freckles. It is my earliest recollection of disliking another person, of feeling vulnerable and afraid and angry and a little bit mean. The boy had breached the false sense of security that I had thus far enjoyed, and he had made me realize that my broken heart was not the only implication of my father's absence. Worse still, he had made me be reminded that my father had, in fact, left me, something I had been getting better at forgetting. I had little defense against that. In fact, all I had in the world in that moment was, "He's one of the helper astronauts."

■ ■ ■

It was around this time that W.T. Thompson, a tiny, sickly kid who looked more like a bug than a second-grader, moved into the house two doors down from me. He did not go to public school because of the severity of his allergies. Instead, teachers went to W.T.'s house, and sometimes a special truck with big hoses went to his house to vacuum all the things that made him sick.

Some days he'd see me walking home from school, and he'd bolt through his front door and race across his yard to stop me in the street.

"Will you play with me?" he'd ask, pushing his gigantic glasses up his nose and trying to catch his breath.

Maybe I thought I was better than him. Maybe I really was just a little meaner than I'd been when I started my new school year. Maybe, for reasons that will make more sense soon enough, I was just plain jealous of W.T.. Whatever my reason, I'd tell him no each time, and I'd barely look in his direction as I passed. Each time was the same. His tiny body would crumple like a puppet whose master has let go of the strings, and he'd stand on the curb watching me walk the distance of the yard that separated our two houses.

Sometimes in the early evenings, I'd watch W.T. from my front porch. I'd watch his father emerge from his car when he got home from work, briefcase in hand, and I'd watch W.T. run down the steps to meet him. Mr. Thompson would wrap his fingers around the top of W.T.'s small head and rock it from side to side as they walked together to the mailbox. Then that hand would fall to W.T.'s slender shoulder and rest there while W.T., on tiptoes, took the mail from the mailbox.

In these moments I began to know with some certainty that I was not a very good kid. It was not a thought I could have written or spoken as clearly as I can today. It was just a feeling growing alongside the mean feeling; if I were a better kid, my mom would not be so tired and irritable all the time, and my father would not have gone, and perhaps we'd be walking together to the mailbox. If I were just a better kid.

■ ■ ■

It was Saturday afternoon. I was racing my bicycle down Wildwood Drive like I'd done at least a hundred times that year, starting at the top of the hill, shoulders hunched, trying to peddle faster than the time before. Airborne, like Evel Knievel, I leapt my own steep driveway and landed in the next-door neighbors' yard, digging in and peddling hard again.

I was just about to exit their driveway, which ran along the side of W.T.'s driveway.

W.T. was hidden from sight behind the rear tire of the neighbor's blue Chevrolet Impala.

And then he wasn't.

On hands and knees, he crawled from behind the car, a magnifying glass in his right hand angled at something he was studying on the concrete.

There was no stopping.

Time tried to slow, tried to throw my bike into reverse, tried to intercept the second, but couldn't as I crashed my bike into the side of W.T.'s head, its rusty fender slicing into his soft, small temple.

I leapt from my bike that was still trying itself to stop, and I hovered over W.T., his small body drawn up into a ball on the driveway like a little bird that had smashed into a big window. He held his head in the bend of one arm and his knees to his chest with the other. He rocked and whimpered, blood leaking from his head back into his baby-like brown curls.

A neighbor ran to W.T. with a rag, pushing me aside. Another pounded on the Thompsons' door, yelling over her shoulder at me, "This would not have happened if you hadn't been riding that bicycle so fast."

"Nancy, move!" one of them yelled as the Thompsons backed out of their drive to deliver W.T. to the hospital.

■ ■ ■

I waited in the kitchen for Mom to get home from work. When I heard our '65 Ford Fairlane float up the driveway and the engine die, I pressed my back against the washing machine, hoping to disappear into its chipped white paint. The screen door whined open and then closed behind her with a sharp clap and then shuddered still.

"Well, Nancy! What in the world?" Mom said when she saw me.

In one fluid motion, she stepped out of her shoes, retrieved a can of salmon and a skillet from the cabinet, clasped the can opener down on the can and began cranking the silver lever.

"So why aren't you playing ball next door? I almost ran over Mike chasing that ball out in the street."

I studied the black linoleum floor, the hole in it made by the rocking of the washing machine. She turned from the waist up and looked at me.

"Nancy?"

"I hurt W.T.," I began. "I hit him with my bicycle."

When I finished with all of the details, leaving out the part about how fast and recklessly I'd been riding and emphasizing one more time that it had been an accident, a bad, awful accident, I waited for her response. There was none. Instead, there was such a silence in the kitchen that I looked up just to see if she was still there. I found her staring at the hole in the linoleum too. The opener in her hand was frozen, the red can clenched in its teeth.

Then with an edge in her voice that cut the silence wide open, she said, "Take your silver dollars. All of them. You take them to that boy's family, and you tell them that you're sorry." She sat the half-opened can on the countertop, then turned

I poured my silver dollars out on the concrete beside me and told myself I was not afraid of Mr. Thompson. I was not afraid of anyone.

and walked away. I watched her disappear down the hall and her bedroom door close behind her.

As I waited on the front porch for W.T. to return from the hospital, I wondered how mean his father was and what he might do to me for busting his kid's head wide open.

I poured my silver dollars out on the concrete beside me and told myself I was not afraid of Mr. Thompson. I was not afraid of anyone. I counted my silver dollars. I stacked them by year. I sat with them the way you sit with the family dog when you know the time has come.

Daddy had collected buffalo nickels before he left us. He had kept them in a fancy cologne box that was black and red. The box was in the attic in his suitcase where it had been since he left. Why he didn't take it with him was something I'd never know. Sometimes I'd go in the attic before Mom got home from work and open the suitcase. In it were my father's perfectly folded clothes, beige button-up shirts on top, white T-shirts beneath, and his box of nickels tucked neatly against the side. I'd trace the stitches that ran alongside the buttons, and I'd pour his nickels out on top of his shirts and count them and worry that he missed them. Then I'd put them back in the box, and I'd put the box back just like I found it, and I'd carefully close the suitcase.

■ ■ ■

On the other side of the screen door, Walter Cronkite had just finished saying *And that's the way it is* on the TV when the Thompsons' car appeared at the top of the hill. Slowly, one by one, I pulled my silver dollars to the edge of the porch step and let them drop back into the jar. Then I picked up my jar and made my way down Wildwood Drive to W.T.'s house.

My knuckles barely made a sound against the wood frame of the screen door, but the inside door opened anyway. Mr. Thompson was bigger up close than he was when he was two houses away, and suddenly I *was* afraid. The more I looked up, the more there was to look up at. He seemed to just keep going up. I stepped back.

Carefully, he pushed open the screen door.

"Nancy, W.T. is going to be fine," he said, smiling. "Would you like to see him?"

"No, sir," I said, only looking halfway up at him and handing him my jar of silver dollars. "They are for the hospital bill. I'm very sorry." I shoved my hands deep into my front pockets and studied the peeling rubber on the toe of one of my blue Keds.

When I heard my silver dollars slide against the sides of the jar, I looked up to see Mr. Thompson holding them up against the sky. He tilted the jar appreciatively. We watched the coins slink from one side of the jar to the other. What was left of the day's orange light seemed to have gathered itself just to lay soft and a little shiny on my silver dollars.

"Nancy, this is a fine collection, but you know we can't accept it."

"My Mom says you have to," I said to my shoes.

He studied me and on the situation. "If I take your silver dollars . . ." He paused. He did not want to take them. "If I take your silver dollars, will you stay and visit just a while?"

I shook my head firmly. I would not.

"If we'll come outside?"

Recognizing the tough spot I was in, I nodded.

Mr. Thompson came outside and began pulling metal lawn chairs into a circle in the front yard, each one complaining a bit. He handed me one and let me help. Mrs. Thompson and W.T. joined us shortly. I looked at anything but them. W.T. kept smiling at me, clearly wanting me to see the helmet of a bandage on his head, but still, I would not look at him.

Instead, I watched Mrs. Thompson talk to Mr. Thompson on the far side of our circle. I watched them like other kids watch magic shows. Her lips were moving, but I couldn't hear her words over the chirping of the neighbor's lawn sprinkler and the crickets, each so loud it was hard to tell one from the other. Mr. Thompson was smiling and looking into her eyes like he thought maybe they were where the words were coming from. In the trees behind them, lightning bugs appeared like Christmas lights.

Mr. Thompson tore the corner off a new bag of Brach's candy corn, stood and handed the bag to me. I handed it to

W.T. without taking any, like I was passing the Communion grape juice and crackers in church.

"You don't like candy corn, Nancy?" Mr. Thompson asked.

"I do," I said. "I like candy corn."

"Then please have some."

I turned and placed my cupped hands before W.T. and then watched in something like disbelief as he poured candy corn so full that two pieces fell into the grass. I let my eyes meet his for just the second that it takes to blink. And then, I got a little braver, stealing glances at the bandage, one glance and then another until I was simply staring at the bandage—the iodine around its edges, how his glasses struggled to clear it, how close it was to the outside corner of his eye. I saw again the blue rusty fender of my bike. Something shifted in me, made the very foundation of me feel compromised. I held my breath, as though that one little breath was suddenly all that was holding me together; as though if I let that breath go either in or out, I might simply collapse like some dilapidated old building.

Worse still, I might cry.

The streetlight flickered, the neighborhood signal to every kid that it was time to be at home.

"I have to go," I said and stood abruptly, my hand still full of candy corn. W.T. smiled up at me, and when he did, the white tape pulled his eye into a slant. I rocked from one foot to the other wanting to fix W.T.'s crooked glasses, wanting to ask him how much it hurt, wanting to say *I'm sorry*, or at least *I didn't mean to hit you in the head with my bicycle*. Instead, I just held onto my little breath that was holding me together.

There is no way for a nine-year-old to know in a moment like this and in the one that will follow that these moments have just become part of them, that this memory will go with them like their own shadow for the rest of their life. A child who knows with certainty that they are bad can't possibly know in a moment like this that they are in fact good and that they are just about to be fastened to that goodness, bonded to it in such a way that it can never come completely undone.

Mr. Thompson rose. "Nancy."

I nodded tight, definite little nods to let him know that I was listening, and I made myself be brave enough to look at him.

"You come back any time," he said. "It was so nice to have your company."

■ ■ ■

The Thompsons moved away not too long after that; they moved to a place where W.T.'s allergies would not be so bad is what I've always told myself. For them, I imagine the story ended there, that it faded like the trim paint on their old brick house.

I still live not far from Wildwood Drive, and sometimes I drive by W.T.'s old house just to remember. The weird place where the two driveways were connected is overgrown now with grass and weeds. In these moments, fifty-two years later, I let myself imagine where W.T. may have gone from here. Because he always seemed so smart to me, I imagine him as president of an Ivy League university. My jar of silver dollars is on one of the many bookshelves I'm sure he has. I imagine him laughing while answering a student's question about how he got that scar on his temple. Perhaps his expression will turn a little reflective, and his pretty eyes behind the big glasses will twinkle when he gets to the part about his father giving the kid some candy corn.

A time or two or more I've gone to the courthouse and searched real estate records for some clue of how I might find the Thompsons. Each time is the same; massive deed books are sprawled out before me, handwritten ledgers going back to 1952, but they are never there, never on that line where they should be.

"Perhaps they were renters," a clerk recently suggested.

Her words settled sadly. Perhaps they were.

And then, just as I've abandoned any hope of ever finding the Thompsons, when any thought of them is far away, a summer evening will fall cool on my damp skin in some distant but familiar way. I almost hear a metal lawn chair whining open, almost feel its prickly, plastic webbing on the backs of a little girl's bare legs.

Other times it's a streetlight in the dead of winter, the way it throws my shadow before me. In it I see her, that little girl walking home from W.T.'s house that night so long ago. I know it's her by the sound of her steps, the rubber soles of her tennis shoes striking the quiet, lonesome pavement. Her fingers are wrapped tight around her little fistful of candy corn that melts warm and sticky in her hand, sweet and buttery on her tongue.

We almost turn and wave. ■

MY MOTHER'S MADAME ALEXANDER DOLL

slept in the posh coffin of a turquoise faux
snakeskin cosmetic box.

Her box was on the top shelf in the closet
of the tiny bedroom I shared with my brother

in our singlewide mobile home,
tucked away where he couldn't reach.

She was precious and porcelain.
To raise her from her casket

was to exhume a jewel from antiquity.
Her skin was impossibly white,

her blue eyes framed by lashes so thick
they must have been made of mascara

or fortified with tears. Her eyes would open only
when I turned her upright. Until then,

she nested in a bed of her own clothing,
coats and muffs and jaunty hats we never wore

in Florida. When I pumped her legs in a scissor-slice,
her head would magically pivot, glancing

to each side of her in an oh so glamorous
safety lesson for crossing a busy street

in a faraway city, somewhere in Russia, perhaps
or New York or Canada, somewhere cold

I had never been. Her blond hair framed her face,
curling only at its ends, not like my brown

untamable mop of curls. Her mouth
was not quite a kiss, not quite a smile,

and she seemed to know a secret
she would never tell me. I knew that I would never

be friends with this perfect girl. If she were real,
she would never speak to me or look my way

as she crossed whatever street in one of the polar cities
that haunted my dreams. But I wanted to *be* her,

to be so special and delicate that to remove me
from my makeup box would be an occasion

no boy would be allowed to interrupt. I wanted
to stride down some foreign boulevard

in a fur coat and hat, cutting the cold air
with my confident legs,

always watching with my ice-blue eyes,
staring down any danger that dare shatter me.
.

SARA JEANINE SMITH

BERNADETTE

Poor sinner, that child trembled at Massabielle when she appeared
in February blue. Wild among roses, some girls threw rocks so hard

we feared that they would stone her. Quartz split wide open
between palm and earth, splattered raw amethyst all over

medieval slabs, smattered shards now all dust saved
in the muddy water. We keep a vial of it on a shelf too high

in sapphire and light. Choice is hard, fluttering between the fear
of stones thrown and the decision to look away, shake our heads,

cover up, level the moving to the stagnant. Sparkling,
uo petito damizelo, we see the sun right through her skin.

Pray for us poor sinners; we can hardly sing. Our mouths drool rusty
clay in harmony, a hymn from childhood, bejeweled with calcium and salt.

CECILIA DURBIN

BOOK REVIEWS

Lucien Darjen Meadows. *Holding On To Nothing.* Spartanburg, S.C.: Hub City Press, 2022. 96 pages. Softcover. $16.00.

Reviewed by Alison Turner

The narrator of Lucien Darjeun Meadows's debut poetry collection *In the Hands of the River*, a boy growing up in an Appalachian coal mining community, tells his story in vulnerable and urgent poems, most of which are no longer than a page. Divided into four untitled sections of free verse stanzas of various lengths, the story both takes place in a "holler," the Appalachian iteration of "hollow" the noun, a kind of valley, and is a form of "holler" the verb, the act of yelling loudly. Through place and speech, the collection remembers the father who left, the speaker's longing for his return, the loneliness of the speaker's mother, the self-harm that brings the narrator closer to his sister, and the violence that follows his young knowing that "When I see a boy [I] think of kneeling." The story is neither linear nor neatly parceled by theme; nothing happens in this holler by direct cause and effect, the way that it is a valley's composition shaped by history that makes it likely to flood, and not the rain.

    The opening poem, "Rust," is placed in front and outside of the collection's four sections like an historical marker, telling us what will happen but not when. Here, where the poem is set, "every plastic swimming pool turns / From its original blue to rust pink in a year or two." These plastic pools hold people, including the speaker: "we lie down / In our plastic pools to rest, to wait—if the rain fell right, / This whole holler could be wiped clear in a night." The holler is an ecosystem of disposability where time is as slow as waiting and as sudden as a flood. The sections following "Rust" live in a similar irony of time. Though the sections are not named, the titles of the opening poem signals a connected story: "First Time," "Second Time," "Third Time," "After." Scanning the book's table of contents, readers see that something will happen again and again, and we ready ourselves, not knowing yet how to feel about "After." This counting becomes a record of suicide attempts accompanied by a number of pounds that track the narrator's decreasing weight and increasing desire to disappear. The simultaneous ambiguity of time and steady tracking of experiences that try to reverse time via smallness and end time via death feels geographical in nature, a swirling of memories in the curves of the valley.

    The speaker in this collection is an outsider to the straight, masculine whiteness that surrounds him, and yet he simultaneously carries the local history of generations. The poem "Tongue" explores what it is "To be red not brown to be / Red but passing white / In this winter-hollow holler." Later, the speaker remembers arriving here as a young boy and hearing a neighbor whisper to his father that they should get a gun, for "Only trees will hear you holler." Later still, no longer new in this place, father and son walk into storms "To howl and holler into lightning," not hiding but watching what will happen: "flashriver, summerflood, wash our holler out." In the second section, the holler becomes a home that is wounded by the father's leaving. In "Clover," the speaker tells his forbidden lover "with ten generations of fathers / Mining and preaching behind you, / Holler is the only home you will ever know". The holler, both the home and the act, is not safe but always promises belonging, as well as the dissonance of waiting for someone to return while knowing they have left.

The third section cuts deeper into this dissonance, the speaker alive but barely, comforted but traumatized. It begins with the poem "Third Time," in which the speaker is reduced to seventy pounds and remembers in short, gasping sentences his suicide pact—completed by one of two—with a lover who told the speaker "it would be easy as slipping. / Into a warm bath. As falling asleep. / To the rocking of my father's truck down. / The holler, the only thing that made me". The holler's promise of comfort makes its violence all the more jarring, like the excisions into mountains that change the terrain and its hold of history. The boy's memories long for "Generations of fathers" who sit on porches "watching / The mountains migrate across the holler" even as "the mountains fall and never come back / Like so many fathers in this coal town". The mountains, made strange by the removal of their heads by mining, are markers of how, when fathers leave, the holler(ing) cannot stay the same.

The final section, whose opening poem promises an "After," offers many possibilities. The narrator has lost a lover, more weight, and the father. And yet he survives these losses, internally as well as bodily. In the final poem, he has found love with a partner, "our horizon beginning". There is no lid over this valley that holds so much love and longing, and the speaker assures us that one day he can leave this violence—which does not necessarily mean leaving the holler. ∎

COPING, OUTSIDE THE LINES

You interrupted this poem
with a hug, asked *will this
make it better or worse?*
My answer—*that depends.*
You're a part of it now.
If you caught me in a night
terror would you shake my
shoulder? Keep me company?
Do you know any jokes that
don't end with me falling flat?
I've built a shrine to heavy
blankets, adult coloring books,
sharpened pencils. You're
free to join. I've coaxed
black and white flowers to life.
I know the general location
of my door knob but not how
to turn. What color would you
make this butterfly? Do you
think it'll fly if we sketch it
a way out? Should we try?

ALISON TERJEK

CELEBRATION OF LIGHTS

Kent, Connecticut, 2021

We stopped believing
as kids but who can't
appreciate eggnog
lattes, or a flush
of rainbow lights
after a short grey
glum day? Weeks
ago we met a friend
also thirty something
also a longtime skeptic
of *family* and *home*
at a fire department
holiday parade. All
three of us balancing
our array of traumas,
hot cocoa cup in one
glove, smartphone in
the other. We snapped
photos as Santa, elves,
grinches on glowing
truck beds, trailers,
and wobbly bicycles
waved and sang to
crowds masked and
unmasked. The entire
event—*past*—within
minutes. We froze
next to our cars after,
searched for satellites.

All anchored to cold
by clear sky, our need
to shiver and share
without trying to make
sense of what doesn't.

ALISON TERJEK

CONTRIBUTORS

Faiz Ahmad is a graduate in Biological Sciences, IIT Madras, India. His work appears in *Poetry Daily, Denver Quarterly, Salamander, Bayou, Poetry Northwest*, and other publications.

Cecilia Durbin lives and writes in Kentucky. Her poetry has appeared in *Screen Door Review* and *Shale*. She holds an MA in English from University of Louisville where she also serves as Managing Editor of *Miracle Monocle*. She divides her professional time at the university between teaching English courses and working for the libraries.

Richard Hague is a fifth-generation Appalachian from Steubenville, Ohio.. He has been on the staff of the Appalachian Writers' Workshop in Hindman, Kentucky and leads a regional online Writers Table from Thomas More University, where he is an Artist-in-Residence. His poems and prose have appeared in *Appalachian Review, Appalachian Journal, Still: The Journal, Northern Appalachian Review, Sheila-Na-Gig*, and many others. A recent collection is *Studied Days: Poems Early & Late in Appalachia* (Dos Madres Press, 2017).

Jason Kyle Howard is editor of *Appalachian Review*. He is the author of *A Few Honest Words: The Kentucky Roots of Popular Music* and coauthor of *Something's Rising: Appalachians Fighting Mountaintop Removal*. His work has appeared in the *New York Times, The Atlantic, The New Republic, Oxford American, Salon, The Nation, The Millions, Utne Reader*, and on NPR.

Jarred Johnson is a queer writer from the Appalachian foothills of Somerset, Kentucky. They live in Wilmington, North Carolina where they are pursuing their MFA in fiction. This is their first prose publication. They are finishing a draft of a novel about Appalachia in the metaverse.

Terry L. Kennedy is the author of the poetry collection, *New River Breakdown*. His previous work appears in a variety of literary journals and magazines including *Cave Wall, Birmingham Poetry Review, and South Carolina Review*, and has been anthologized in, most recently,

You Are the River: Literature Inspired by the North Carolina Museum of Art. He currently serves as the Director of the MFA Writing Program at UNC-Greensboro where he edits *The Greensboro Review.*

Sarah Ladd is a Kentucky journalist from West Kentucky who now lives in Louisville. She earned her MFA from Spalding University in 2022 and undergraduate degrees from West Kentucky Community and Technical College and the University of Kentucky. She works as a health beat reporter for the *Kentucky Lantern*, a nonprofit news service in Frankfort. In her free time she loves hiking with her rescue dog, Ronon.

Dorothy Neagle is a Kentuckian who lives and writes in New York. Her poetry has appeared in many journals and anthologies, including *Painted Bride Quarterly, Epiphany,* and *Pedestal*. Her first book of poems has been selected as a finalist or semi-finalist for multiple publishing contests. Her nonfiction has appeared in *Memoirist, The Nasiona,* and *The Dead Mule School of Southern Literature.* Read more from her at dorothyneagle.com or @sentencesaremyfave.

Josh Nicolaisen taught English for twelve years and is currently an MFA candidate at Randolph College and the owner of Old Man Gardening LLC. He lives in New Hampshire with his wife, Sara, and their daughters, Grace and Azalea. He is a Pushcart Prize nominee whose work has recently appeared in *Colorado Review, So It Goes, Northern New England Review, Backlash, Concision,* and elsewhere. Find him at www.oldmangardening.com/poetry.

Ann Pancake grew up in Summersville and Romney, West Virginia. She is the author of two short story collections, *Given Ground* and *Me and My Daddy Listen to Bob Marley*, and a novel about mountaintop removal mining, *Strange As This Weather Has Been*, which was one of *Kirkus Review*'s Top Ten Fiction Books of the year, won the 2007 Weatherford Prize, and was a finalist for the 2008 Orion Book Award and the 2008 Washington State Book Award. She has also received a Whiting Award, an NEA grant, the Bakeless Prize, and a Pushcart Prize.

Ashley Danielle Ryle's work has most recently appeared in *Zone3, Cheat River Review, Cordella,* and *Raleigh Review*. Her chapbook

Fetching My Sister is with Dancing Girl Press, and she was a recipient of a brief residency through the Kentucky Foundation for Women in 2014. She earned her MFA from West Virginia University and currently resides with her husband in central Pennsylvania.

Sara Jeanine Smith lives in Pensacola, Florida. She is a mother of two daughters and an associate professor of English at Pensacola State College. She enjoys kayaking with dolphins for company and singing in bars. Her poems have appeared in *South Florida Poetry Journal, Barely South Review, Pigeonholes, Roanoke Review, Psaltery & Lyre, Hurricane Review,* and other publications. Her chapbook entitled *Queen and Stranger* was published by USPOCO Books in 2019. See more of her work at sarajeaninesmith.com.

Burnside Soleil grew up in a houseboat on the bayou but these days is a pilgrim in New Orleans. His work has appeared or is forthcoming in *Kenyon Review, New England Review,* and elsewhere.

Alison Terjek is a writer and mental health advocate living in Northwestern Connecticut. She spends her weekends outdoors where she searches for peace and inspiration in the mountains. Her poetry has appeared previously in *Watershed Review, The Healing Muse, RiverSedge, Peregrine, Appalachian Review* and elsewhere.

Jeff Tigchelaar's poems appear in *Agni, Atlanta Review, Beloit Poetry Journal, Best New Poets, CutBank, Fugue, Harpur Palate, Hunger Mountain, The Laurel Review, The MacGuffin, New Ohio Review, North American Review, Pleiades,* and *Tar River Poetry,* as well as on *Verse Daily.* My first collection, *Certain Streets at an Uncertain Hour* (Woodley Press), won the Kansas Authors Club's Nelson Poetry Book Award.

Alison Turner grew up in the mountains of Colorado, where she learned to endure large amounts of time in inclement weather waiting for buses. After completing degrees at Colorado University-Boulder, the University of Alberta, Bennington College, and the University of Denver, her work has been published in *Western American Literature, Archivaria, American Archivist,* and *Community Literacy Journal,* among other journals. In the winter of 2023, her first collection of short stories will be published with Torrey House Press.

Emry Trantham is a poet and high school English teacher. She lives with her husband and daughters in Western North Carolina, where she captures the landscape through both words and photographs. Her poetry appears in numerous journals, including *EcoTheo, Tar River Poetry, Cold Mountain Review, Booth,* and *Appalachian Review.*

Jeff Wallace is a graduate of Indiana University's MFA in Fiction program. He is currently an Associate Professor of English at Southern State Community College, serving the Appalachian communities of southern Ohio. He lives in that area, with his wife and two children. His work has been published previously in *Appalachian Heritage, New Southerner, Still: The Journal,* among other publications.

Nancy Luana Wilkes grew up in Decatur, Georgia where she lives today and where many of her personal essays, like this one, are set. She is a graduate of the Naslund-Mann Graduate School of Writing at Spalding University in Louisville, Kentucky and was a runner-up in the Atlanta Writer's Club 2021 Rick Bragg Prize for nonfiction. She is also a contributing feature writer for the *Atlanta Journal Constitution.*

Printed in the USA
CPSIA information can be obtained
at www.ICGtesting.com
CBHW081357010324
4804CB00008BA/974

9 781469 677446